The REVOLUTIONARY WAR *in*
BENNINGTON
C O U N T Y

BENNINGTON COUNTY, VERMONT

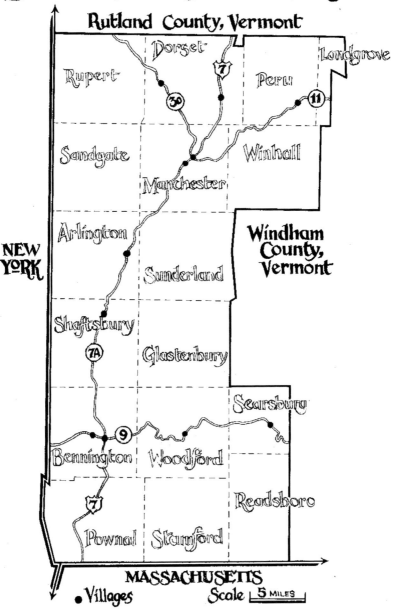

Rutland County, Vermont

Rupert

Dorset

7

Longrove

Peru

11

30

Sandgate

Winhall

Manchester

Arlington

NEW YORK

Sunderland

Windham County, Vermont

Shaftsbury

7A

Glastenbury

Searsburg

9

Bennington

Woodford

7

Readsboro

Pownal

Stamford

MASSACHUSETTS

• Villages

Scale |__5__ MILES |

BENNINGTON COUNTY, VERMONT

Bennington County was formed in 1781 by the independent Vermont. This map shows the current seventeen towns in the county.

RICHARD B. SMITH

The REVOLUTIONARY WAR *in*
BENNINGTON
COUNTY

A HISTORY & GUIDE

THE
History
PRESS

Published by The History Press
Charleston, SC 29403
www.historypress.net

Cover image: *Prisoners taken at Battle of Bennington, August 16, 1777.* Painted by Leroy Williams in 1938 for the Bennington Museum through the Works Progress Administration (WPA). The painting portrays the scene in Old Bennington with the different American participants and some of the seven hundred British prisoners who were captured at the Battle of Bennington. General John Stark from New Hampshire is shown riding a horse. In the far background is Mount Anthony in Bennington, and in the right rear is the Walloomsac Inn that is still in existence today. The full twelve- by six-foot mural is on display at the Bennington Museum. *Courtesy of the Bennington Museum.*

All images are courtesy of the author unless otherwise noted.

First published 2008
Second printing 2010
Third printing 2011
Fourth printing 2012

Manufactured in the United States
ISBN 978.1.59629.444.8

Library of Congress Cataloging-in-Publication Data

Smith, Richard B.
The Revolutionary War in Bennington County : a history and guide / Richard B.
Smith.
p. cm.
Includes bibliographical references and index.
ISBN 978-1-59629-444-8 (alk. paper)
1. Bennington County (Vt.)--History, Military--18th century. 2. Vermont--History-
-Revolution, 1775-1783--Campaigns. 3. Bennington, Battle of, N.Y., 1777. 4.
United States--History--Revolution, 1775-1783--Campaigns. 5. Bennington County
(Vt.)--Tours--Guidebooks. I. Title.
E230.5.V3S65 2008
973.3'443--dc22
2008018154

CONTENTS

CONTENTS

ACKNOWLEDGEMENTS

Many historical societies were helpful in providing manuscripts, documents and books: the Manchester Historical Society, Dorset Historical Society, Bennington Historical Society, the Manchester Historic Association (New Hampshire), Connecticut Historical Society and the Washington County Historic Society (New York). Paul Carnahan at the Vermont Historical Society was also supportive.

Besides historical societies, other institutions and organizations were valuable resources. The Fort Ticonderoga Association and Museum (Ticonderoga, New York) provided many published articles. The George A. Russell Collection of Vermontiana at the Martha Canfield Library and the Bennington Museum were informative. The Vermont Division of Historic Preservation in Montpelier was a useful resource. The Old First Church (Bennington) provided some background literature, photos and information. The National Life Group in Montpelier graciously provided images from its Old Vermont series. The United Empire Loyalist Association (Canada) also offered information.

Many individuals played important roles in the preparation of this book: Nancy Andrews, Emmy McCusker, Art Gilbert, Judy Harwood, Martha Heilmann, Vicki Jerome, Verrall Keelan, Shirley Lawrence Letiecq, Brian Lindner, Peter and Sue Palmer, Karl Pfister, Cynthia Schultz, Cassie Stewart, Terry Tyler, Paul Williams and Debbi Wraga.

In addition to keeping a tradition alive, the Ethan Allen Days Committee has been supportive: Laine Akiyama, Lisa and Al Gray, Carrie Howe, Ed Knight, Paula Maynard and Anne and Ron Weber.

Individuals at Hildene, in addition to preserving history in a lively and interesting way, provided information: Gary Sloan, Rose Marie Simard, Bob Guarino (who also owns a historic home) and Dick French (who has also given tours of Manchester Village). Curator Brian Knight offered his assistance in the form of various documents.

Special thanks must go to Tyler Resch, librarian of the Bennington Museum, for his aid—he led me in the right direction and checked some of my facts. His own books were a great source of information. Bill Budde at the Russell Collection was supportive and even researched some probate records.

Bill Badger graciously shared some of his experience in historic preservation and architecture to help create the rendering of the Marsh Tavern from historic documents.

Thanks to Colleen Plimpton for reviewing preliminary drafts of the manuscript.

Don Martin helped produce the line art in this book

My wife, Sharon, reviewed some of my work—she always makes Vermont interesting to people taking her Backroad Discovery tours.

Living in Manchester, Vermont, has also given me a great appreciation over the years for all those individuals and institutions that have been part of the region's historical preservation efforts. In addition to being a member of several historical societies, it has been an honor to serve as president of the Manchester Historical Society and a trustee of the Vermont Historical Society.

INTRODUCTION

This historic guide is designed for the leisurely traveler who wants a broad understanding of the two major events that occurred in what is now Bennington County, Vermont, in 1775 and 1777. (Bennington County was formed in 1781.) This guide also tries to lead the traveler along the same routes taken by the participants in these events in order to view the same sites seen by them over two hundred years ago.

In 1775, Ethan Allen marched north from Bennington, mustering Green Mountain Boys along the way, and then captured Fort Ticonderoga for the first victory of the American Revolution.

In 1777, the British recaptured Fort Ticonderoga and then marched south to try to split the colonies and win the war. They aimed to replenish their supplies by capturing the storehouse in Bennington. The resounding defeat of the British by John Stark from New Hampshire and Seth Warner from Bennington County at the Battle of Bennington denied the British their supplies and led to the defeat and surrender of the British at Saratoga, which is accredited as being the major turning point of the war.

Due to decades of preservation efforts by individuals and institutions, many of the homes, routes and sites associated with these events not only still exist, but they also exist in historic settings. Of course, the beauty of Vermont without any billboards provides a wonderful travel experience.

For those interested in a more in-depth study of the many towns, houses, sites or people involved with these historic events, many references, including websites, are provided.

1775

THE MARCH NORTH: ETHAN ALLEN'S CAPTURE OF FORT TICONDEROGA, AMERICA'S FIRST VICTORY

1775 ~ THE MARCH NORTH
May 10, 1775 ~ First American victory ~ Capture of Fort Ticonderoga.

To Fort Ticonderoga

Rupert

Dorset

NEW YORK

(36)

(7)

(11)

Manchester

Sunderland
Ethan's brother Ira
lived here

Arlington
Ethan's cousin,
Remember
lived

Baker
here.

Shaftsbury
Galusha's Tavern

(7A)

(9)

Old Bennington ~
Catamount Tavern
(Green Mountain Boys'
Headquarters ~ Ethan
Allen lived next door.)

(7)

MASSACHUSETTS
Scale ⌐ 5 MILES ⌐

ETHAN ALLEN'S MARCH NORTH

Ethan Allen started his epic journey in Bennington. On May 10, 1775, he captured Fort Ticonderoga in the first American victory of the American Revolution. The capture was accomplished three weeks after Lexington and Concord.

THINKING THE IMPOSSIBLE

Capturing Fort Ticonderoga

The first victory of the American Revolution for the Americans was the capture of Fort Ticonderoga on May 10, 1775, by Ethan Allen, three weeks after "the shot heard round the world" at Lexington and Concord. Majestic and massive Fort Ticonderoga, located on the western shore of hundred-mile-long Lake Champlain, had been called another Gibraltar, and it guarded the historic invasion and trade route from Canada south to the Hudson River Valley. Fort Ticonderoga, with its dozens of cannons and brilliant design, enabled, in 1758, about thirty-eight hundred French troops to repulse an attack by about fifteen thousand British troops during the French and Indian War.

How then, seventeen years later, could Ethan Allen from Bennington, Vermont, think that he could march seventy miles north and capture Fort Ticonderoga? There were no large cities or towns, like in Connecticut or Massachusetts, from which to draw recruits. Bennington itself only had a total population of about 550 people. Even if he recruited people, training them on such short notice would be difficult. Allen was asking those who were essentially farmers, for the first time, to take offensive action—not defensive action—against the British empire to protect their land and homes. With only 200 to 300 recruits and no cannons, what made Ethan Allen cross Lake Champlain, certain that he could capture the fort?

The answer to these questions and many more can be found in the history of Vermont and its early settlers. Bennington had, in fact, only been settled fifteen years before the capture of Fort Ticonderoga. It was, at the time, the northern frontier.

EVENTS LEADING TO THE SETTLEMENT OF BENNINGTON COUNTY

Although many had traveled through the area known today as Vermont, it was basically an unsettled no man's land—a vast wilderness. New York had claimed most of the area based on the charter granted by Charles II to the Duke of York in 1664. New York interpreted this charter to mean that the Connecticut River north of Massachusetts was the eastern boundary of New York State. At times in the past, Connecticut and Massachusetts, as well as the Dutch and Native Americans, had laid claims to parts of this area. However, wars in the west, Native Americans protecting their hunting areas, French influences in the northern area and other factors kept Vermont from being settled.

In 1716, a seemingly insignificant event occurred that would be the basis for the formation of Vermont and Bennington County years later. In colonial America, after lands were occupied, it would not be uncommon for a survey to show that one state had inadvertently taken land from another. One way to handle this issue peacefully was for the offending state to give "equivalent land" to the other state as compensation. In one such event, Massachusetts gave Connecticut 107,793 acres of land. Connecticut, in turn, on April 24–25, 1716, decided to raise money by holding an auction for these equivalent lands. One of the successful bidders in the auction included an individual from Massachusetts named William Dummer. The importance of this purchase was that 43,943 acres of this land happened to be on the <u>west</u> side of the Connecticut River, about where present-day Brattleboro is located.

Then, in 1724, because of increasing concern about Native American raids into Massachusetts from the north, the Massachusetts legislature authorized the building of forts along its northern border. William Dummer, who had become acting governor, chose this piece of land <u>west</u> of the Connecticut River as the site of the fort. The fort was called Fort Dummer.

1741 to 1749
The Crown's Rulings Lead to the Creation of the "New Hampshire Grants"

In 1741, King George II returned New Hampshire to its royal province status, no longer under Massachusetts authority and with its own governor. That new governor was American-born and Harvard-educated Benning Wentworth. During this period, the border with New Hampshire was redrawn, and Fort Dummer was now north of Massachusetts's northern border. Massachusetts saw an opportunity to rid itself of the maintenance costs of Fort Dummer as threats of Native American raids were decreasing at this time. The king bought the Massachusetts arguments and gave responsibility of Fort Dummer to New Hampshire.

Using the precedents that Fort Dummer was now the responsibility of New Hampshire, that the Massachusetts/New Hampshire borderline had been altered by the Crown and that Connecticut and New York had agreed on a western boundary for Connecticut of twenty miles east of the Hudson River, Governor Wentworth claimed that the Massachusetts–New Hampshire border went to within twenty miles of the Hudson River. Wentworth therefore claimed that he could charter towns and grant land west of the Connecticut River all the way to twenty miles east of the Hudson River. Wentworth also used other dubious reasoning, such as claiming that the original charter given to the Duke of York should be east to the Connecticut River, but the charter didn't clearly indicate the word "river." Wentworth, in general, claimed that the 1664 King Charles II charter to the Duke of York did not express definitively the territory to be covered.

On January 3, 1749, Benning Wentworth, in a very aggressive move, chartered under a New Hampshire grant the first town west of the Connecticut River and located it twenty miles east of the Hudson River. To show even more arrogance, he chose to use his name, calling it Bennington. This was the first of what would be known as the "New Hampshire Grants," which eventually became the state of Vermont. There was no established New York government rule in this essentially unoccupied area.

Wentworth's actions were an affront to the New York leaders; however, Wentworth sensed that he was pushing the limit of his authority. He wrote to the governor of New York, claiming that he was willing to have the Crown decide if he had the authority to issue these grants. He didn't charter any more towns for two years, but since New York didn't really do anything to stop him and the Crown didn't make any declaration about where the eastern boundary of New York was located, Wentworth resumed chartering towns in 1753. Another indication of how shaky Wentworth thought his authority was to grant lands was the extremely low prices he offered—the grants might not hold up over time. One estimate valued land in "the Grants" at one one-hundredth of the value of land in Maine and one four-hundredth the value of land in Western Massachusetts.

The formula was the same for all of the chartered towns. The towns were about six miles by six miles and had about sixty-four initial proprietors (mostly from southern New England), who either bought or were given plots of land in these new towns. These proprietors were basically speculators who hoped to resell the land to settlers. Bennington had sixty-four proprietors and these proprietors would sell land rights to individuals. Of course, Wentworth kept some land for himself—some lots on the Bennington town plan clearly show the initials "BW"—and he made many murky deals for which he was later chastised. He also set aside land for the church. Wentworth named many towns after people or places in England to gain favor in his land-granting efforts. (For instance, Rupert was probably named after the English Prince Rupert.)

In all of what is now Vermont, there were only a few granted towns from 1749 to 1760, with three of these towns being in today's Bennington County. However, these towns were essentially only towns on paper. Because of the ongoing French and Indian War, these lands were basically unsettled. In reality, Bennington stood alone on the western border, twenty miles from the Hudson River and many miles west of established New Hampshire.

The boundary line at the time did not just delineate which provincial government had control where, but it also divided two economic systems. New York tended to have large manors with tenants working the land. New England tended to have small farms with the owners working the land themselves. New Hampshire was chartering its towns to proprietors, many of whom had never been in the Grants, and instead of settling there themselves, they would sell smaller lots to individuals who wanted to work their own land.

The New Hampshire grant system attracted people from New England who wanted freedom and local autonomy but couldn't afford land in their own states. As we will see, when land is at stake, people will fight and die to protect what they have worked to build.

1760

Bennington County Settlement Begins in Earnest

A Land Once of the Abenaki and Other Groups

Settlement of Bennington County really didn't begin until Montcalm was defeated in Montreal and it appeared that the French and Indian War was coming to an end. The New Hampshire Grants were located between the English settlements in southern New England and the French settlements in the north, including Canada. Once this war was settled, there would not be Native American or French raids to endanger settlers. The Abenaki people were active in various parts of Vermont prior to settlers moving up from southern New England. (Officially, the war was concluded with the signing of the Treaty of Paris in 1763.) Settlers felt more secure, so they started coming to the Grants in earnest. With the war winding down and without real resistance from New York or the Crown, Governor Wentworth became active and issued many more grants—especially in 1761, when he chartered over fifty towns in Vermont.

The leader of the first settlers of Bennington was Samuel Robinson, who came to the area in 1761. Although he was unusual in that he was a proprietor who actually came to settle rather than sell his land, he was, in many other ways, very typical of the settlers who would move to Bennington and the other towns. During the second half of the 1750s, Robinson, who was from Hardwick, Massachusetts, served in four campaigns of the French and Indian War in the Lake George–Lake Champlain area. In 1757, he returned to Hardwick to raise troops to fight the French, but he found that Hardwick men were disgusted with the British. In 1758, Robinson was part of the disastrous frontal assault by the British on Fort Ticonderoga, and then in 1759 he was part of the victorious capture of Fort Ticonderoga by Jeffrey Amherst, putting Fort Ticonderoga into British hands.

As Robinson traveled back and forth to these military events, he became more enamored of local control and sense of community and rebelled against the rigid life of a soldier. More importantly, during his travels he went through the unoccupied area where Benning Wentworth was granting land, and he liked what he saw. Conversely, he did not like things in Hardwick and other towns in Massachusetts and Connecticut, where there was more encroachment on local autonomy.

As a military person, Robinson had some money, so in 1760 he started to buy land in the Grants. In 1761, he sold his holdings in Hardwick and led thirty families to Bennington. The site of Samuel Robinson's first house—a log cabin—is clearly marked in what is now Old Bennington.

Vermont represented, for many years, a true frontier life that was very different from life in New England towns that had been founded over a hundred years earlier (Hartford was founded in 1636, Boston in 1630). In addition to the lure of cheap land, there was a religious upheaval taking place in Massachusetts and Connecticut that would add to the incentive to move to Bennington and the newly chartered towns. Hundreds of Congregationalists in Massachusetts and Connecticut were part of a struggle within the church between the "New Lights" and the "Old Lights." The old order of the Old Lights was afraid of the separatists—so much so that in many towns the New Lights were being harassed. George Whitefield and other evangelical preachers were encouraging their followers to have a direct relationship with God. The movement was called the "Great Awakening." This desire for religious freedom and cheap land encouraged independent-thinking people to move from southern New England to the northern frontier.

Samuel Robinson was a purist type of Congregationalist. He was one example of the kind of people who wanted to settle in a new area for their version of religious freedom. There was religious diversity in Bennington County, but that diversity was usually by town, not within towns.

Geography helped the settlement of Bennington County. There were many convenient routes to this new northern frontier. The route traveling up through Western Massachusetts (the beautiful Berkshires) from

Connecticut and Eastern Massachusetts made the lure even better. There were east–west routes through Bennington: west for trading in Albany and east through the Green Mountains to Brattleboro, New Hampshire and Boston. There were routes north to the Champlain Valley. Bennington was nestled in an area between the Taconic Mountains and the Green Mountains known as the Vermont Valley.

King George III took over the Crown in 1760 at the age of twenty-two. With many other issues to consider, the young monarch didn't give much attention to this local issue in the colonies involving land disputes between New York and New Hampshire, so the settlers kept coming. As a result of the end of the French and Indian War, the chartering of new towns and the opportunity for cheap land and religious freedom—all in a setting of New England–style local autonomy—there was rapid settlement of towns in present-day Bennington County beginning in the 1760s. For example, Bennington (1761); Arlington and Shaftsbury (1763); Manchester (1764); Rupert (1765); Sunderland(1766); Dorset (1768); Landgrove (1769); Sandgate (1772); and Peru (1773).

THE KING RULES IN 1764 IN FAVOR OF NEW YORK TITLEHOLDERS
But Forgets about the Current Settlers, Creating More Trouble

Finally, fifteen years after Benning Wentworth's first town charter of Bennington in 1749, on July 20, 1764, King George III issued an order in council that the west bank of the Connecticut River was to be the boundary between New York and New Hampshire. The ruling favored New York, but the use of the phrase "to be" begged the question: What about the current landowners in Bennington County? These strong-willed settlers had brought their families to the area and cleared the land they thought they had bought from the Crown via its legitimate governor, Benning Wentworth. New York took the position that current landowners from the New Hampshire Grants would have to be regranted in some way and, in effect, they would pay for their land twice. New Hampshire sympathized with the Grants landowners, but upheld the king's ruling.

Bennington County, because it was next to New York, became the focal point of the growing dispute with New York. Farmers, who had done the arduous task of clearing land and building homes and sawmills, were not about to pay for their land twice. In addition, they were concerned about being under New York authority with its manorial system.

SAMUEL ROBINSON'S WIFE AND LOG CABIN, BENNINGTON
Robinson was the leader of the first settlers in Bennington. He built a log cabin on today's Monument Avenue. When he went to England in late 1766 to try to resolve the land issue with New York, his wife was left behind to fight off wolves from their cabin. A marker designates the spot of the log cabin. *Reprinted by permission of National Life Group. Artwork by Roy Heinrich. Published in* Life *and the* Saturday Evening Post, *1943.*

Many of the existing settlers in 1766 were hoping to solve this dispute peacefully. Therefore, in late 1766, Samuel Robinson went to England to plead the settlers' case, leaving behind his wife and family to fend off wolves from their cabin in Bennington.

Settlers had a rough life on the northern frontier, and ultimately they were willing to fight for the chance for a better life. On July 24, 1767—three years after ruling that the boundary of New York and New Hampshire was <u>to be</u> the Connecticut River—the privy council issued a second order in council warning that New York, "upon Pain of his Majesty's highest displeasure," was *not* to issue any further grants "until his Majesty's further pleasure is known." The Crown again did not resolve the problem.

Robinson became ill with smallpox and ended up dying in England in late 1767, but his efforts had not been totally in vain. New York did refrain from granting land for a couple of years, but then it resumed issuing grants (patents) of its own, and many of these conflicted with the original New Hampshire land and town grants.

Late in 1769, one such grant conflict involved the town of Shaftsbury in Bennington County. John Small owned land under a New York grant and Josiah Carpenter owned the same land under a New Hampshire grant. This was an important test case, as it would be one final opportunity to settle everything peacefully. The dispute was billed as part of the "ejectment trials" to be held in Albany under New York courts.

1769‑75

Ethan Allen and the Green Mountain Boys

ETHAN ALLEN ARRIVES

The Albany ejection trials, to be held in June 1770, required someone to coordinate the defense of the Grants settlers. Many of the nonresident proprietors (the original people who bought the land rights from the governor) were speculators in the New Hampshire Grants and had a lot to lose if New York was granted title. The proprietors met in Connecticut and chose the man to help them—Ethan Allen.

They had the right man. Allen had been to the Grants previously, hunting and exploring. He was born in 1738 in Connecticut and had family in the Grants, including two cousins, Seth Warner (born in 1743), who lived in Bennington, and Remember Baker (born around 1737), who was in the Arlington area. Allen had organizational skills and was a good orator. He was intelligent, loved the frontier and was a born leader. He loved to drink with his friends. Although he liked to travel and was away from home often, he was also, surprisingly, a family man who wanted to provide for his wife and family and eventually bring them to the Grants.

Allen lived in Bennington from 1769 to 1775. However, using Bennington as his base, he traveled considerable distances over the next five years and became familiar with the people and the land, especially on the west side of the Green Mountains. He would travel as far north as Burlington—over a hundred miles away. Allen was the right

ETHAN ALLEN'S BENNINGTON HOME

The house in the foreground has been attributed to Ethan Allen while he lived in Bennington. The courthouse behind the Allen house is no longer there, but the Old First Church still exists as Vermont's "Colonial Shrine." The Old Burying Ground is now where the home and the courthouse were located. The original house may have had alterations prior to this picture being taken. Ethan Allen was a resident from 1769 to 1775. A marker now indicates where the home was located. *Courtesy of Vermont Historical Society.*

combination of forceful leader and somewhat of an intellectual and writer, as can be seen today in preserved manuscripts. He was essentially an honest and fair man, and he was evidently good to have around. George Washington wrote about Ethan Allen: "There is an original something in him that commands admiration."

There are many physical descriptors for Ethan Allen in the literature: he had "awesome physical power," could "run a deer to death without getting a sweat up" and could "fell an ox with a single blow of his massive fist"; he was "a large frame man," "robust" and so forth. He was over six feet tall, which was tall for those days. Unfortunately, history is not blessed with a painting of Ethan Allen, as no authenticated image exists. Even the statue of Ethan Allen in Washington is a composite impression of an artist. The statue in Montpelier is generally accepted by many as being close, but it is still a speculative likeness.

THE EJECTMENT TRIALS

Allen immediately started working on the ejectment trials. It was determined that he needed the proper documents from the governor of New Hampshire. To show his willingness to travel for a cause, he rode over 125 miles from Bennington to Portsmouth, New Hampshire, to see the governor, John Wentworth. The original governor, Benning Wentworth, had resigned under pressure in 1766, and his nephew took over the governorship. Although John Wentworth offered encouragement and gave Allen the documents he needed, Wentworth advised him to get a good lawyer and suggested a man in New Haven, Connecticut. Off Allen went to New Haven, and then to Albany. Even with lawyers and titles to the land from a governor of the Crown, the trial was over before it started. The New York judge (who owned land in the Grants under a New York patent) would not allow the titles from New Hampshire grants to be used as evidence, even though the grants had been issued under the king's seal.

After losing, bold Allen told the New York lawyers,

"The gods of the valleys are not the gods of the hills."

When asked what this meant, Allen responded, "Come to the Grants and I'll show you what I mean."

THE GREEN MOUNTAIN BOYS FORM IN BENNINGTON

By 1770, Bennington had become the main town in what is today Bennington County. It had formed a separatist Congregational church (1762, the oldest in Vermont) and had enticed a preacher, Reverend Jedediah Dewey, to settle there. Dewey built a house in Bennington in about 1763 (it is still standing today). A meetinghouse (1763–1765) was built by the congregation (the site is marked today). Bennington also boasted an inn (Walloomsac, still standing) and the home of Ethan Allen, as well as a tavern known as Fay's Tavern or the Green Mountain Tavern (built ca. 1767–69) that would later become famous as the Catamount Tavern. As evidenced by these buildings, the settlers, in the years leading up to 1770, had built a nice little community in Bennington through hard work. They were not going to give this up to New York authorities without a fight. (As will be discussed later, they would not give up their freedoms to the British Crown either.)

FIRST MEETINGHOUSE, BENNINGTON
Built in 1763–65, Ethan Allen attended a service of thanks given here after the capture of Fort Ticonderoga and Battle of Bennington prisoners were held here. It was replaced in 1806 by the current Old First Church, Vermont's "Colonial Shrine." A large tablet with inscriptions marks the spot in the middle of the Old Bennington Green. *Courtesy of Old First Church, Bennington, Vermont.*

Ethan Allen returned to Bennington and called for a "convention" to be held at the Catamount Tavern, which had become the political and social center of Bennington and was conveniently located almost across the street from where Ethan Allen lived. Operated by Stephen Fay, the Catamount had a big room appropriately called the "Council Room." The favorite drink at the Catamount Tavern was the Stonewall—very hard cider with rum—and tradition says that Ethan Allen could down more than anyone in the Grants. The tavern was a square, unpainted building of two and a half stories. In front was a stuffed Catamount, snarling in the direction of New York. Ethan Allen claimed at one time that the tavern had the "best liquor west of the mountains."

It was in this setting that, after having lost the ejection trials before they even started, Allen convinced the "convention" that now was the time to start using force. Using his imposing six-foot presence, combined with his organizational skills, confidence and leadership skills, he elicited agreement to form a militia group that had no real legal authority. Unlike some other militia groups in New England, this was a voluntary group. According to tradition, after the New York governor heard about this group, he said that he would drive the "Bennington mob" (as he called them) back into the Green Mountains—thereafter, the group was called

THE CATAMOUNT TAVERN, BENNINGTON
Also known as Fay's Tavern and the Green Mountain Tavern, it served as the headquarters of the Green Mountain Boys, as General Stark's headquarters before the Battle of Bennington and as a meeting place for the Vermont Council of Safety. Ethan Allen left from here to capture Fort Ticonderoga. It burned in 1871. *Picture may have been taken by Calvin Dart. Courtesy of Vermont Historical Society.*

the Green Mountain Boys. The Catamount Tavern in Bennington would be the headquarters of the Green Mountain Boys for years to come.

The Green Mountain Boys elected Ethan Allen their colonel commandant. Allen organized them into five companies by vicinity (town). Three of the key initial leaders of the companies were from Bennington County: Seth Warner (from Bennington), Robert Cochran (from Rupert) and Remember Baker (from Arlington).

These Green Mountain Boys were primarily farmers (over 60 percent) and over 70 percent owned land when they joined. According to one estimate, around 43 percent originally came from Connecticut and about 40 percent originally came from Massachusetts. Most had only basic education and about 39 percent were in their twenties. Allen was born in 1738, so he was about thirty-two when he was elected colonel commandant of these volunteers with no official status.

There is no clear indication of how many original Green Mountain Boys there were. It appears that there were at least three hundred, and maybe up to one thousand, all over the Grants. The main concentration of Green

Mountain Boys was naturally along the disputed border with New York. They had no uniform, but some did put an evergreen twig in their hats. Ethan Allen, being a little flashier, may have had "fancy, gold-braid epaulettes" and a big sword, but nothing else is known with certainty, except that he did use a horse. Over time, people in formal Vermont military units would be informally referred to as Green Mountain Boys. Even today, National Guard units are informally referred to as Vermont's Green Mountain Boys.

The original Green Mountain Boys were angry. They had purchased land in good faith from a governor of the king and now some other governor was trying to take their land. If one looks at the Bennington County countryside and pictures the effort that was required to clear land—first, cutting trees and then removing stumps and rocks over a five-year period—one might begin to understand the desire to fight. Conversely, the settlers from New York who were trying to come to the Grants also felt that they had bought their land legitimately from a representative of the Crown.

Although the purpose of the Green Mountain Boys was force, the group used it very carefully, relying mainly on intimidation, harassment, surprise and threats. Ethan Allen was smart enough to avoid bloodshed— none from the Green Mountain Boys lost their lives between 1770 and 1775. Humiliation, intimidation and scare tactics were powerful weapons. On occasion, the "Boys" did burn houses, however.

Ethan Allen was smart politically and would not rely totally on the force of the Green Mountain Boys to establish their just rights to the land. He wanted the common farmer in New York and New England to sympathize with his cause, so he made sure that he had their support. He wrote letters to the Crown, as well to the *Hartford Courant*, to plead his case.

THE INTIMIDATION PERIOD
Five Years of Using Military Tactics to Intimidate

For the next five years, practically every attempt by New York authorities to take the land of the Grants would be met with some form of opposition from the Green Mountain Boys. Starting in 1771, there was not a month that went by without some form of confrontation. These confrontations became military training for the group of citizen farmers who were standing up for their rights by being organized, having the ability to respond quickly, being disciplined enough to follow a leader and believing they could win against bigger forces.

Although being directed from Bennington, the Green Mountain Boys' actions were all over the west side of the Green Mountains. For instance, in May 1771, word reached Bennington that a New York surveyor was in Pittsford (about sixty miles north of Bennington in Rutland County). Ethan Allen immediately assembled a small group of the Boys and set out on horseback to Pittsford. The surveyor left after hearing of the Boys' approach.

A very significant confrontation occurred in 1771 that showed many of the military skills of the organized Green Mountain Boys. The high sheriff of Albany County, Henry Ten Eyck, Esq., set out from Albany (thirty miles away from Bennington) with a posse of over three hundred men to eject James Breckenridge from his farm, which was in today's North Bennington. Through a network of spies and friends, word reached Bennington that this posse was coming. Alerted, the rebels quickly raised people to wait for Ten Eyck. They were armed and strategically placed in a military fashion: some in a house, some in a field, some on a ridge and so forth. Ten Eyck couldn't get the entire posse to advance because some were farmers who sympathized with the Grants farmers. No one was hurt, and Ten Eyck returned to Albany. Ten Eyck never expected a resistance to be organized so fast.

Another confrontation occurred when Ethan Allen, Remember Baker, Robert Cochran and about six Boys went to Rupert (Bennington County), with a lot of musket waving, and burned the partially finished cabin of a New York settler. The New Yorker returned to New York, saying that Allen had boasted of being able to raise hundreds of Boys on short notice. Just north of Rupert is Poultney, and Allen had spent considerable time there because of some land he owned. Only Ira (Ethan's younger brother) and Remember Baker may have known more than Ethan Allen about this whole area. Poultney is on the road from Bennington to Fort Ticonderoga.

Surprise was another tactic used often by the Green Mountain Boys to intimidate. Dr. Samuel Adams of Arlington was "taken by surprise," carted off to the Catamount Tavern and put in a chair to hang for a few hours until he agreed to the demands of the Green Mountain Boys to not support New York.

As a result of these activities, Ethan Allen and several others (Baker and Cochran) were declared outlaws by New York, and a reward was offered for their capture. In defiance, and partially in humor, Allen, Baker and Cochran offered a reward, in turn, for James Duane, who had been the lawyer for New York at the ejection trials. The reward called for bringing Duane and Kemp (New York attorney general) to the Catamount Tavern, and it showed how Ethan Allen was standing up for all the towns to the north. (All three who signed the reward poster were from Bennington County.)

HIGH CHAIR TREATMENT, BENNINGTON
The Green Mountain Boys used embarrassment and intimidation methods against their enemies. They surprised a Yorker sympathizer, brought him to the Green Mountain Tavern in Bennington (later known as the Catamount) and hung him in a chair for a while. *Reprinted by permission of National Life Group. Artwork by Roy Heinrich, 1943. Published in* Time *and the* Saturday Evening Post, *1953.*

£25 Reward

Whereas James Duane and John Kemp of New York, have by their menaces and threats greatly disturbed the public peace and repose of the honest peasants of Bennington and the settlements to the northward, which peasants are now and ever have been in the peace of God and the King and patriotic and liege subjects of George III. Any person that will apprehend these common disturbers, viz: James Duane, and John Kemp and bring them to Landlord Fay's at Bennington, shall have £15 reward for James Duane and £10 for John Kemp paid.

Ethan Allen
Remember Baker
Robert Cochran
Dated Feb. 5, 1772

Another incident in 1772 that showed how quickly the Boys could respond occurred on March 21. A New York sheriff named Munro (who lived in Shaftsbury) came during the night into the house of Remember Baker in Arlington, captured him and put him on a carriage to Albany. Munro probably thought no one could help because Allen was many miles to the south in Bennington. However, Baker's wife, Desire, escaped and woke up neighbors. Within an hour, there were twelve people from the Arlington-Bennington area chasing the carriage. They caught up with Baker in Troy and freed him. Organized and quick action was becoming common in Bennington County. (A side note is that Baker lost his thumb in the scuffle and that turned out to be the worst injury in the whole Grants conflict.)

Ethan Allen was even willing to take on the British, not just New York State's sheriff. In May 1772, word reached Bennington that British troops were coming up the Hudson River with the New York governor to oust the Grants settlers. Allen sent a spy, his brother Ira, to Albany (right in the heart of the action) to get the facts. At a meeting at the Catamount Tavern, some hesitated to take on the British, but Allen prevailed and elaborate military action plans were made to defeat the British. In the end, no action was needed, as the troops were going west to relieve some forts in the Niagara area of New York. The Boys, however, had practiced military planning and had used spies to get information.

A more formal affront to New York was a convention in Manchester in March 1774 at Eliakem Weller's tavern (still in existence as a private home) in which the convention said that inhabitants should be ready to help one another defend themselves against the New Yorkers.

In March 1775, the "Westminster massacre" occurred on the eastern side of the Green Mountains. There was a major disturbance involving a group defying New York authority that ended in the death of two settlers. At Ethan Allen's direction, Robert Cochran showed up in twenty-four hours with over thirty Green Mountain Boys to help the settlers against New York. There was surprise that so many people could be raised so quickly.

By the early spring of 1775, Ethan Allen and the Green Mountain Boys had become an organized unofficial military group, based at the Catamount Tavern in Bennington but covering all of Bennington County and towns to the north and east. They were armed and had experience in confrontations. They sent out spies. They knew how to surprise. They knew how to operate at night. They knew (especially Ethan Allen) Bennington County and lands to the north and east, as well as the roads

ELIAKEM WELLER TAVERN, MANCHESTER
Built in 1774, the Green Mountain Boys met here. There was also a convention here
in March 1774 that voted to support the Green Mountain Boys against New York land
claimants. It is now a private residence.

and the settlers. They seemed to always send the right number of Boys
for the mission. They could produce a contingent of Boys at a moment's
notice at various locations. They were motivated to defend their land,
their religion and democracy on a very local level. There was no question
that their leader was Ethan Allen. They had friends and the sympathies
of farmers in New York and New England. Most importantly, Ethan
Allen had the respect of farmers throughout Vermont who would follow
him on his word in a moment's notice, no questions asked.

Ultimately, the Crown had created this military group. Had the Crown
understood the impact of giving responsibility of Fort Dummer to New
Hampshire, and had it been careful about the boundaries with New York,
Connecticut, Massachusetts and New Hampshire, Wentworth would not
have been given the opening he needed to justify the first test grant—
Bennington. Had the Crown not waited fifteen years (from 1749 to 1764)
to decide that the New York–New Hampshire border was "to be" the
Connecticut River and then been vague about the status of existing settlers,
there might not have been the rush of settlers into previously unoccupied
Bennington County. Had the Crown not waited three more years to issue a
cease and desist order for new New York grants "until the Crown's wishes

are known" instead of resolving the issue of the existing settlers, there might not have been the fighting for land until a decision was made on rights.

The Crown didn't realize that what it thought was a local issue between the governors of New York and New Hampshire was the catalyst for the creation of an organized force that would consider the Crown the enemy—not New York. The Crown was also more concerned with other events during this time period, such as the Intolerable Acts and the Boston Tea Party. Ethan Allen, in his writings and oratory, more and more equated the Grants' struggle for liberty against New York with the colonists' struggle for liberty against the Crown. It was a way-of-life issue—not a border dispute.

THE AMERICAN REVOLUTION AND ETHAN ALLEN'S BIG DECISION

On April 19, 1775, a group of British soldiers marched to Concord through Lexington to try to capture a colonial storehouse at Concord about twenty miles west of Boston. The colonists and the British were fighting. It appeared to be open rebellion against the Crown. This "shot heard round the world" reached Allen when he was in the eastern part of the Grants. He immediately rode back to Bennington and the Catamount Tavern for consultations.

If this was open rebellion, then the colonists would need the heavy artillery available at Fort Ticonderoga—about seventy miles north of Bennington on the western shore of Lake Champlain, opposite Shoreham, in what is now Vermont.

It seems that many in the colonies had thought about the need to capture Fort Ticonderoga. In fact, earlier that year, John Brown—a Yale graduate and lawyer from Pittsfield in Western Massachusetts—was on a mission to Canada to determine, in part, the feelings of the Canadians should hostilities break out with England. He was accompanied by Pelag Sunderland of Manchester who also spoke Abenaki. On March 29, 1775, Brown wrote to the committee of correspondence in Boston and included the following sentences:

> One thing I must mention, to be kept as a profound secret.
> The Fort at Ticonderoga must be seized as soon as possible,
> should hostilities be committed by the King's troops.

Brown concluded his letter by even suggesting that the people in "the New-Hampshire Grants" (present-day Vermont) were the "proper persons for this job."

Ethan Allen, however, had a big decision to make. To try to capture Fort Ticonderoga would mean, if the British won the war, that all the land grants would be wiped out by the victorious Crown and New York would be favored. Others were also urging caution because, if the settlers remained loyal and the British won the war, the Crown might rule in their favor, as it had already, in 1767, told New York to stop issuing new grants. Additionally, there was, of course, the feeling that perhaps all of these colonists-Crown issues could be settled peaceably without the need for true open rebellion. Simply put, there were a lot of people who were loyal to the Crown in Bennington County towns. The plaque in the center of the Old Bennington green states it correctly: Who do you fight—"the oppressive measures of New York" or "the overwhelming power of King George"? People's right "to alter or abolish injustices" was now becoming acceptable.

Another issue was the question of how the others in the colonies would react. If they attacked Fort Ticonderoga (on New York soil), would New York—a colony that had put a bounty on Ethan Allen and others—react favorably? How would Connecticut, New Hampshire and Massachusetts react? After all, the Green Mountain Boys had not been elected by the people (although they elected their officers), and they had no real authority.

What if the Green Mountain Boys were the cause of permanent rebellion rather than the potential for peaceful settlement? Ethan Allen was not in favor of showing caution at this moment. He was able to convince people that the issue was right versus wrong and not to wait. As he said, to "explore futurity" was "unfathomable."

Time was an issue. If the British had time to reinforce the fort, either internally or with help from Canada, it would be lost forever, and the trade route and military route down the Champlain Valley and the Hudson Valley would remain in British control.

Ethan Allen's Mind Was Made Up
He Was Going to the Side of Liberty and Freedom

Around May 2, by express horse, Ethan Allen's brother, Heman, who was in Hartford, Connecticut, for land meetings involving Vermont, arrived at the Catamount Tavern with news that a group from Connecticut and

Massachusetts was headed to Bennington to seek Allen's help in capturing Fort Ticonderoga from the British. It had only been thirteen days since Lexington and Concord.

A group of Patriots from Massachusetts and Connecticut did arrive in Bennington between May 3 and 5. The Connecticut group of about sixteen people had begun in Hartford, and another thirty-nine or so recruits joined the group in Western Massachusetts (the Berkshires). The group had borrowed money from the Connecticut treasury and was actually going to reimburse people for some expenses of the trip.

Their route to Bennington was basically along what is now the Route 7 corridor from Stockbridge to Pittsfield and then Lanesboro and Williamstown. The group entered Vermont in the Bennington County town of Pownal. From logs, it does not seem that this group actually stopped in Pownal. After years of research in the early twentieth century, Robert O. Bascom produced a study that indicated that at least two persons from Pownal were with Ethan Allen at Ticonderoga. (This is a helpful list to determine who from each Bennington County town was with Ethan Allen at Fort Ticonderoga.) Captain Samuel Wright was actually one of the first to enter the fort with Ethan Allen. Another study by Donald A. Smith (no relation to the author) mentioned, on the Pownal Historical Society home page, that there were over twenty-five Green Mountain Boys in Pownal, among whom Captain Samuel Wright is listed. Another person from Pownal who was with Ethan Allen at Fort Ticonderoga was Josiah Dunning, who enlisted as a volunteer with Captain Samuel Wright.

Why were so few Green Mountain Boys from Pownal with Ethan Allen at the fort? The first explanation may be that the Connecticut/Massachusetts contingent was in a hurry to get to the next town, Bennington, and did not want to stop and recruit in Pownal. They also may not have known who these Boys were or where these Boys lived. Recruits may have lived quite a distance from the main road, and the group may have wanted to keep the mission a secret. They also knew the Boys would follow Ethan Allen, not them. There could have been more people from Pownal involved, but the various lists disagree on where individuals lived. For instance, a Captain Gideon Warren is listed by the historical society as being from Pownal, but the list by Bascom of people who were with Allen at Fort Ticonderoga includes a Captain Gideon Warren from Hampton, New York (fifty miles to the north and just over the New York border near Poultney, Vermont). For speed, Allen may not have gone south to recruit, but instead raced north as fast as he could to recruit.

On the Route 7 corridor, just after crossing the Pownal/Bennington town line, there was a tavern strategically built about two hundred yards before a split in the road. Monument Avenue bears off to the left up to Old Bennington. The Route 7 trail went farther north into the current downtown area of Bennington, where there were houses like the Safford House (still visible). The Connecticut/Massachusetts group probably would have passed that tavern (built in 1770) and taken the route west up to the Catamount Tavern.

Arriving at the Catamount Tavern in Bennington (Old Bennington today), this initial contingent had some "orders" from members of the Connecticut Committee of Safety (not officially from the council itself) to seek the help of Ethan Allen and his Green Mountain Boys in capturing Fort Ticonderoga. The Connecticut contingent included notable Patriots Edward Mott, Noah Phelps, Levi Allen (Ethan's brother) and Samuel Parsons. From Massachusetts came James Easton of Pittsfield who supplied most of the Massachusetts men and John Brown who had been to Canada earlier in the year. (As a side note, John Brown was related by marriage to a bookseller in Connecticut named Benedict Arnold.) The Massachusetts contingent had said that it would be difficult to raise men in the Grants, so they brought enough people to help, but not enough to give away the mission.

After further discussion and consultation at the Catamount Tavern to achieve unity, it was decided to capture Fort Ticonderoga. Ethan Allen was ready and he would lead the expedition. His Green Mountain Boys were organized in the towns and they would follow Allen religiously and without question. He was the defender of their way of life and had proved it over the last five years. Since Bennington was only a small town of about 560 people spread over thirty-six square miles, there was no fort with troops ready to be called up. Green Mountain Boys would have to be recruited as they moved north. It would be Ethan Allen's decision as leader to decide who and where to recruit and not to endanger secrecy.

As Allen walked out of the Catamount Tavern in May 1775 to begin mustering his Boys for this epic march north, he would have seen the Walloomsac Inn, Nathaniel Brush's house, the Old Burying Ground and Parson Jedediah Dewey's house, all of which are still there today. If he had turned around and looked at the Catamount Tavern (which burned in 1871), it would have had the same unpainted look as the Walloomsac Inn has today. Ralph Earl of Bennington showed these buildings in a painting done in 1798. The painting is a little stylized, but if the building in the front, the Tichenor House, and one or two others that weren't yet built in 1775 are deleted, it gives a good sense of

"Allen needs you at Ti!"

"ALLEN NEEDS YOU AT TI"
A runner is recruiting farmers (Green Mountain Boys) to go with Ethan Allen to capture Fort Ticonderoga. That's all the runner had to say—there was complete trust in Ethan Allen. The gun (without bayonet) and clothes were the type used at the capture of Fort Ticonderoga. The illustration also depicts the urgency.
Reprinted by permission of National Life Group. Artwork by Herbert M. Stoops. First published in Saturday Evening Post *and* Time, *1947.*

how small Bennington was at that time. It was only eight years prior that settlers were protecting themselves against wolves in downtown Bennington. Samuel Robinson's cabin, portrayed in the image on page 20, is shown in the painting across the street from the big white house, just to the right of the center of the picture.

From this little town of Bennington, one of the most exciting adventures in American history was about to begin. Ethan Allen was about to march seventy miles north from the Catamount Tavern, recruiting Green Mountain Boys along the way, and attack Fort Ticonderoga in the first offensive military action by the colonists in the American Revolution. He knew he could recruit Green Mountain Boys who were essentially farmers that wanted independence and were willing to fight for it. Over the last

OLD BENNINGTON

This is a 1798 painting by Ralph Earl. Although the layout of Old Bennington is a little different, if Isaac Techinor's house (left front) and the small building to the right were removed, it would give a sense of the small size of Bennington in 1775 and 1777. *Courtesy of Bennington Museum.*

five years, the Green Mountain Boys trusted Ethan Allen and were willing to drop everything to join him if he asked them to do so.

Although, looking back, it seemed like a risky venture, Ethan Allen never seemed to think he could not accomplish the feat. He had never been in the fort. There were rumors that the fort had fallen into disrepair, but Allen didn't really know for sure whether the walls could be breached. He didn't know if word had reached the fort that there was rebellion or if it was prepared for an attack. His was an even more remarkable feat when one considers that the Green Mountain Boys had no uniforms (except maybe a twig in their hats), no cannons, few bayonets, no tents and few provisions.

The Green Mountain Boys did have some advantages. They were organized up and down Bennington County and towns to the north. They knew and respected Ethan Allen. They were aware of the importance of time, secrecy and surprise. They had no artillery to drag. They could move fast and they knew the Native American trails. Ethan Allen knew the territory—he had held off New York for five years. All he had to do was find the farmers and tell them they were needed.

THE MARCH NORTH

Speed, Secrecy, Trust and Organization

Ethan Allen moved quickly. Five years of military operations had prepared Allen and the Green Mountain Boys for this action. Guards were sent out to block roads to and from Fort Ticonderoga to keep the march a secret and to prevent word of Lexington and Concord from reaching the fort. Ethan Allen left the group that was still coming into Bennington to muster some of his Boys between May 3 and 5. Because he had a horse and experience traveling great distances, he was capable of spreading the word over a large area. His plan was to have people that could not go with the group immediately meet on May 8 at Castleton, about fifty miles to the north.

Bennington provided four notables to the expedition according to Robert Bascom's list. One Green Mountain Boy who was with Allen at Fort Ticonderoga was Dr. Jonas Fay, the son of the owner of the Catamount Tavern, Stephen Fay. Jonas would later draft the Vermont declaration of independence. His gravestone is clearly visible in the Old Burying Ground, next to Ethan Allen's homesite and walking distance from the Catamount Tavern. Josiah Fuller of Bennington also went along, evidently as a surgeon's mate, and he may have actually been paid by Connecticut for his services on the expedition. The other notable person was Seth Warner, whose house was on the west side of town. Although he would join Ethan Allen at Fort Ticonderoga, Warner was apparently in the north at the time with his cousin, Remember Baker. Ethan Allen sent word ahead, telling Warner and Baker to meet him for the expedition. Samuel Herrick is also considered to have been associated with Bennington, although Bascom does not list a town for him in 1775.

In Connecticut or Massachusetts, it had been decided not to have a large group marching north so as not to give away the purpose of the trip. It is reasonable to assume that people may have taken different routes, and we know that some would march later and become spread out. We are blessed that some people wrote about the journey afterward, but one of the people from Connecticut, Epaphras Bull, kept a short diary that turned out to be the only known contemporary log (written while on the trip) of the entire expedition.

Some did have horses that account for the successful traveling of hefty distances over long periods of time. There are indications of "carts," which may have been used to carry some provisions, but these carts were probably used only for short periods. Some in the group had money to pay for provisions and lodging along the way. This also helped keep secret the mission, since it looked like they were just travelers headed north—it was not uncommon for armed hunting parties to go north in search of game.

At 9:00 a.m. on Friday, May 5, a contingent left the Catamount Tavern and headed north on what would now be the Historic 7A corridor up the Vermont Valley. The old road going out of Bennington went up Harwood Hill, which is now Historic 7A, and then north. The group would have to cross the Walloomsac River that meanders north and west into New York.

SHAFTSBURY

The first stop on the road north is Shaftsbury (about six miles north of the Catamount Tavern). The population in Shaftsbury in 1775 was only 500, similar to Bennington's 585. Like Bennington, this was a recently organized and settled town. Just ten years before, in 1765, it was estimated that there were 18 residents. The western border of Shaftsbury abuts the New York border, so this was an active area for the Green Mountain Boys.

One of the groups arrived at 10:30 a.m. at "Mr. Galusha's tavern." In an hour and a half, they had traveled the six miles from Catamount Tavern. (That is about four miles per hour, indicating some may have had horses.) The inn referenced in the diary of the troops moving north is no doubt the David Galusha Inn, which is listed on the National Register of Historic Places as being built around 1775–76. The Galushas themselves are a well-known family in Shaftsbury, as well as in Vermont. David Galusha's Inn is on the

THE DAVID GALUSHA INN, SHAFTSBURY
Some of those people traveling north to capture Fort Ticonderoga stopped at David
Galusha's Tavern. The inn was built around 1775. The original structure may have also
been built over a period of a year or two. David Galusha was a Green Mountain Boy,
fought in the Battle of Bennington and was part of Seth Warner's regiment. The house
is now a private residence.

current Route Historic 7A. Jonas Galusha came to Shaftsbury to live in 1775,
and it appears that his older brother, David, probably came at the same time.
(Jonas went on to be a nine-term governor of Vermont.)

Revolutionary war "taverns" took several forms. Some were rather large,
like the Catamount Tavern, and also had meeting rooms and sleeping
quarters for guests. In some cases, there might be an inn for sleeping and
the tavern might be across the street or next door. Occasionally, the "inn" or
"tavern" was in someone's house. Since Bull's diary indicates stopping at "Mr.
Galusha's tavern" in May, and the "David Galusha Inn" was built around
1775–76 and the Galushas had apparently just come to the area in 1775, it is
possible that the tavern was very small at the time and was added on to later.
Operating immediately as an inn or tavern was a quick way of getting money.

There is no indication that anyone from Shaftsbury was with Ethan
Allen at Fort Ticonderoga. In the interest of speed and secrecy, the group
apparently kept going rather than spend time recruiting in Shaftsbury.

ARLINGTON

The next town on the march north was Arlington, which presented a fascinating challenge. Towns in Vermont were settled in many cases by religion. For instance, Bennington had its "Separate" Congregationalists and Shaftsbury had a core of Baptists. Many Episcopalians settled in Arlington, and the Episcopalians were very close to the Church of England, so you tended to have a lot of Tory sympathizers there. Even today, there is a street called Tory Lane in Arlington. Arlington, therefore, presented a challenge; namely, to get through town without suspicion so the British at Fort Ticonderoga could not be warned. (A small twist in the religious issue was that Ethan Allen was an Episcopalian living in Bennington. Later in life, his religious beliefs became unique.)

The group going to Fort Ticonderoga arrived at Arlington on the same day—Friday, May 5—at noon, and one of the contingent actually "borrowed a gun" at "Mr. Holly's." A search of documents gives no conclusive information on who "Mr. Holly" was or where he lived. (Actually, many Arlington records of the era are missing, possibly due to the town clerk, who was a Tory.) Based on the spellings of the various towns in these diaries, it is conceivable that "Mr. Holly" was actually Mr. Hawley. From Historic 7A west on 313 (Water Street) along the Batten Kill (River), about one mile toward New York, there was the tavern owned by Abel Hawley, built in 1773. (The house still exits today as a private residence.)

Hawley's tavern was unique in that it was a meeting place for both the Tories and the Green Mountain Boys. Ethan Allen would have known this house because Abel Hawley was on one of the military committees of the Green Mountain Boys. "Trials" were also held there by the Green Mountain Boys, after which the offending person was sent on his way to New York, down the Batten Kill. At the time, many people had not declared themselves Tories, as there was not really a major rebellion. It had only been two weeks since Lexington and Concord over two hundred miles away. Since the group arrived at noon on a Friday in a town of only 320 people in 1775, it is possible that one or more of the group went to Hawley's and then returned to their journey without raising any suspicion.

One of the early settlers of Arlington in 1763 was Ethan Allen's cousin, Remember Baker, who built a gristmill on the East Arlington/Sunderland line (about a mile east from today's Historic 7A in the opposite direction of the Hawley House). Remember Baker was one of the most fervent Green Mountain Boys.

On May 5, 1775, Remember Baker was in the north near Burlington, and Ethan Allen had already sent a messenger to have Baker meet the group when it arrived north. Therefore, there was no need for the group to leave the main road to recruit Baker. East of Historic 7A, there is also a parallel route north from Arlington. By going east toward Baker's gristmill in East Arlington, the road meets Sunderland Hill Road, which goes north. There is no conclusive documentation, however, that any in the group went up Sunderland Hill Road, although it is possible.

SUNDERLAND

After leaving Arlington, the expedition passed through the northwest corner of Sunderland without stopping. There is no one specifically identified in Bascom's study as being from Sunderland. Some people, like Ethan Allen's brother Ira (born in 1751), are identified, but without an associated town. Ira, as did Ethan, definitely lived in this area and played a big role from here later. It is not clear whether Ira was living here during the month of May 1775. Child's *Gazetteer of Bennington County* indicates that Ethan Allen had actually lived in Sunderland before residing in Bennington. Ira had come to the Grants in 1770 and was a surveyor, so he knew Vermont and traveled frequently. His role in the capture is not well documented. Ira Allen owned land in Sunderland, east of what is now Historic 7A.

MANCHESTER

The next stop on the march north was Manchester. From the time this group arrived in Arlington at noon to the time they arrived in Manchester at "4 O'Clock," it had taken four hours to go about eight to ten miles. There is no indication of how long they stopped to rest along the way.

Primarily, people from New York—Amenia to be precise, just over the New York border—settled Manchester, unlike the other towns on the march to Fort Ticonderoga. These settlers enjoyed individual ownership of land, as opposed to the New York manorial system—a main reason these "Yorkers" settled in Manchester. For a town estimated to have only 350 people in 1775, Manchester tended to be a more open town and therefore had more taverns and inns. The church was actually built after some taverns.

The March North: Speed, Secrecy, Trust and Organization

The logs indicate that the group "dined," not just ate, in Manchester. (One can still get a good meal in Manchester today.) Totaling over fifty people, it is possible that the group split up in Manchester or was in the town at staggered times. Dining also could have been done at private homes or taverns. Coming up what is now Route Historic 7A, the group would have passed many places to eat, and many are still in existence today. There is the Latrobe House (just off Historic 7A), the farm of Samuel Rose (one of the first settlers of Manchester), the Inn at Ormsby Hill, the Jeremiah French house and the Weller Tavern. Then there was the Marsh Tavern, the predecessor to the Equinox Hotel. The other French house was there in 1775. (It is now the 1811 House bed-and-breakfast.)

Of all those houses mentioned, logic would seem to indicate some may have "dined" at the Eliakem Weller Tavern (see image on page 31), which is the same tavern that held a convention in 1774 to support cooperative efforts among the settlers against New York land claims. Eliakem Weller's daughter married Benjamin Roberts. Benjamin Roberts was the son of John Roberts (one of the first settlers of Manchester), who provided the most members of any family to participate in the seizure of Fort Ticonderoga. The Roberts family consisted of five boys and two girls. The father John and all five of his boys were identified as having been with Ethan Allen at Fort Ticonderoga. Two of the boys, William and Peter, settled in Dorset. It is recorded that General Christopher Roberts (John Roberts's fourth youngest son) was one of the first to enter Ticonderoga. Christopher Roberts was also brother-in-law to Pelag Sunderland of Manchester, who also went to Fort Ticonderoga. (Pelag spent time in both Manchester and Rutland. On the lists of who was with Allen at Ticonderoga, no town was listed for Pelag Sutherland.) Three of the Roberts brothers would also fight later in the Battle of Bennington. Stephen Smith of Manchester was also with Ethan Allen at Fort Ticonderoga.

Manchester represents an important fork in the road going north. A traveler or Green Mountain Boy could go north to the mustering point of Castleton by essentially taking one of two routes. One route would have been to continue in the Vermont Valley up the center of the state on the Route 7A (then 7) corridor to Rutland (about thirty miles) and then going west to Castleton (adjoining Rutland). Another route takes advantage of the break in the Taconic Range starting in Manchester. The traveler at Manchester could go northwest to Castleton via what is now Manchester West Road to Dorset and Rupert via the Mettewee Valley. There are map indications that the actual route north on West Road may have been a little farther west up the foothills as West Road approaches Dorset. This latter route is the fastest to the mustering point of Castleton. The marchers chose this latter route to Castleton.

DORSET

Three of the company went on to Dorset via the Mettawee Valley, but they did not stop in Dorset. The remainder of the company stayed in Manchester. The route taken through Dorset was probably on what is today Dorset West Road, which had the Cephas Kent Tavern on it. The Cephas Kent Inn, located today in the vicinity of the old Cephas Kent Tavern, was built in 1775, but it may have been built as early as 1773.

Across from the tavern was what is today called Kent Meadows. Tyler Resch, in his very thorough book, *Dorset: In the Shadow of Marble Mountain*, states that "legend" has it that Ethan Allen camped on Kent Meadows on his way to Fort Ticonderoga. Supporting information for listing the entire Kent Historic District on the National Register of Historic Places includes the statement: "tradition" has it that Ethan Allen camped here. Also, just before Kent Meadows is what is today called the "Ethan Allen Spring." The spring is listed on the state list of historic places, but without significant supporting information. Kent Meadows in 1775 may not have been cleared, so it is possible that people were camping near the Cephas Kent Tavern or farther south by the spring. Of the six Roberts family members who were with Ethan Allen at Fort Ticonderoga, two lived in Dorset and the other four were in Manchester. It could have been that some of the family members camped or mustered on Kent Meadows to meet the others in the group who were taking this route.

Although three of the marchers went through Dorset, it is possible that part of the company that remained in Manchester came up and camped at Kent Meadows. Old maps also indicate that there were roads from the east (for instance, Danby), from where Ethan Allen could have come after trying to muster troops. Allen then could have gone up to Rupert, the next town, where it is recorded that he did join the group.

If a group were to camp in Dorset, it would have probably been on Kent Meadows near a known road, a tavern, flatland and a spring. The other possibility is somewhere along the current Route 30 to the east, but this area had considerable wetlands. There were, however, houses in the area. One of these is the Deacon John Manley house made of marble.

It may have been built before 1775 and therefore was a place to stop or rest. It is visible today next to the quarry, whose sign states that it is "the oldest" quarry in the United States, having opened in 1785.

If a group did camp in Dorset, it may have been small, given the total number of people who came from the area and were with Ethan Allen at Fort Ticonderoga. Not only did Dorset, in 1775, have a population estimated at about 250 spread out over thirty-six square miles, but some areas were on the other side of Mount Aelous. Dorset is somewhat different than Arlington, which seemed to have a main road running down the center.

Just up West Road about a quarter of a mile was a mile marker that may have been there when the marchers came by in 1775. This mile marker is visible today in the Dorset Historical Society, and there are conflicting dates as to when it was placed there.

Farther up on West Road is Foote Road, which leads up and off to the left for half a mile at a much higher level than West Road and then goes back to meet West Road just before Rupert. There are indications that Foote Road was actually the main road before the parallel West Road was improved. Having houses such as the Amos Field House (circa 1775) and others on Foote Road would support the tradition that Foote Road was the main road.

RUPERT

The first group of three arrived in Rupert and lodged there on the night of May 5. That meant that, since the group left Bennington at 9:00 a.m., these Patriots had traveled about thirty miles in one day to Rupert. It would seem that, for at least part of the time, they had to have been on horses.

The Mettawee Valley route passes through the northeast section of Rupert (now East and North Rupert) before leaving Bennington County. Rupert's major individual contribution to the Fort Ticonderoga capture was Robert Cochran. He was a captain with the Green Mountain Boys before the Revolution. He came to Bennington in 1768, but then moved to Rupert.

Conversely, Rupert (which only had about 230 people in 1775) also had many Tory sympathizers. One of the Tories left with many town records, so documentation is not complete. We know that some of the contingent stopped and stayed at "Smith's," which could have been Martin Smith's tavern, but documentation is inconclusive on the location of the "Smith's" that is referenced. Another map produced by Meritt Barden in 1928 shows a Smith family living nearer to what could be today's Route 30 in east Rupert. Enoch Smith had three sons, Thaddeus, Hiram and James, and all were living at this spot, according to the 1790 census. Since Thaddeus was eighty-two when he died in 1857, he would have been born in 1775—Enoch would have been at least around twenty at that time. It is also possible that part of the group stayed on what is now Route 30 for a few miles and stopped near what was then called Mill Brook and is now Hagar Brook. Jonathan Eastman had a farm and a cabin there. His oldest son, Enoch, would have been about twenty-seven in 1775 and shows up on the militia roles with Martin Smith; he also served with Seth Warner. Perhaps "Smith's" was actually Eastman's house, with Smith staying there as a friend, and the marcher went to Smith's place later or merely thought it was Smith's home because he was there. The Hagar Brook and the farm area are visible today. (Hagar Brook was also where Harmon Mint coined money for the future independent Republic of Vermont in the 1780s.) Further research is needed to determine exactly where the group stayed in Rupert, but we may never know.

Ethan Allen joined the group in Rupert for an unknown amount of time. The rest of the group came up to meet at Rupert. Allen could have been mustering Green Mountain Boys in the outlying farms in almost any direction. Robert Cochran's farm was to the west, by the New York border. Allen could have mustered with others back at Kent Meadows in Dorset and then joined the group in Rupert. Some of the group continued on from Rupert and some stayed to refresh their horses.

At Rupert, the group heard from scouts that potentially eighty British soldiers were guarding Fort Ticonderoga, but "*they [were] repairing the Fort.*" Even with only eighty men in Fort Ticonderoga, the fact that the British were repairing it suggested that they might already have known that the group was coming—the walls might have no longer been breachable. There was concern within the group that they would be able to take Crown Point Fort (just north of Fort Ticonderoga), which was much smaller, but that they would not be able hold it, as reinforcements could arrive faster from Canada than from the colonies. The Boys were facing a "dilemma." Fort Ticonderoga could not be taken and the smaller fort (Crown Point) could not be held, so was there really any point in continuing on? Even with this bleak outlook for success, the expedition continued north.

THE CAPTURE OF
FORT TICONDEROGA

America's First Victory

Speed was important so as not to give the British time to reinforce Fort Ticonderoga. From Rupert, the group left Bennington County and went up through Pawlet, Wells, Poultney and then on to Castleton. From May 5 until the May 8 mustering at Castleton, the journey covered fifty miles.

At Castleton, there was again a conference. Edward Mott, a steady man from Connecticut, was formally elected chairman of the "Council of War." Ethan Allen was elected field commander. The military-type skills he had learned after five years of fighting New York had already become evident. From all the way south in Bennington, Allen had been able to muster the expedition to Castleton with complete secrecy. His other military skills would soon surface. Allen needed information about the condition of Fort Ticonderoga, the number of people there and their general state of readiness. To this end, Noah Phelps (who had come through Bennington from Connecticut) was sent to the fort to spy on the British, pretending to be a woodsman looking for a haircut. Allen also realized that, while he knew the east side of Lake Champlain, he was not familiar with the fort itself. (A good leader knows his limitations.) He convinced the father of a local boy—Nathan Beman, who had played at the fort often and knew it intimately—to let his son guide them to the fort.

Another task was logistical: getting boats to cross Lake Champlain. Allen's knowledge of the area indicated that in Skenesborough (current-day Whitehall, New York) there were boats owned by Phillip

Skene. Bennington's Samuel Herrick and about thirty people were sent west to Skenesborough to get boats. In another military maneuver, Allen sent another group as a backup to get boats in case the Skenesborough mission failed. Boats were eventually secured by telling people that they were on a hunting party at Hand's Cove. Allen went to Hand's Cove in Shoreham on the night of May 9 to wait for boats with his men.

Unfortunately, only a few boats arrived. Estimates vary on how many people were at Hand's Cove in the very early morning of May 10, but most estimates seem to be in the two hundred to three hundred range. Regardless of how few people there were, Ethan Allen decided to proceed. However, due to the scarcity of boats on the morning of May 10, only eighty-three men actually crossed Lake Champlain to attack the fort. (Some say that Allen may not have counted himself.) The others at Hand's Cove, with Seth Warner in charge, would come over in the second wave. Thanks to information from the spy Noah Phelps and the young guide Nathan Beman, Ethan Allen felt comfortable attacking. At dawn, he entered the fort and caught the British garrison completely by surprise. Epaphras Bull, in his diary, wrote that they entered the fort with a "shout," using the Green Mountain Boys' intimidation tactic to make the enemy think there were more men than there actually were. There was no bloodshed. Ethan Allen, in his narrative, said that when he told the British commander, Captain de la Place, to surrender, the commander asked under what authority. Ethan Allen replied:

In the name of the great Jehovah and the Continental Congress.

On May 10, 1775, Ethan Allen and fewer than three hundred men (mostly Green Mountain Boys) accomplished the first victory of the American Revolution just three weeks after Lexington and Concord and five days after leaving the headquarters of the Green Mountain Boys at the Catamount Tavern in Bennington, Vermont, seventy miles to the south. They took the first prisoners in the Revolution. The cannons at Fort Ticonderoga were captured, as was rum, which was used to celebrate in true Green Mountain Boy style. Accounts vary due to a lack of records and the failure to count the men who retrieved boats or guarded the roads, but in total over two hundred men had been mustered. As the plaque by the New York State Education Department at the entrance to Fort Ticonderoga reads:

Ethan Allen and his Green Mountain Boys captured Ticonderoga in a surprise attack, May 10, 1775.

ETHAN ALLEN'S CAPTURE OF FORT TICONDEROGA
The original painting in 1848 was by Alonzo Chappel and depicts Ethan Allen and
Captain de la Place, the British commander. Ethan Allen was guided to the fort by a
youth, Nathan Beman, *Courtesy of National Archives.*

MORE DETAILS ON OTHER NOTABLE PARTICIPANTS AT FORT TICONDEROGA WITH BENNINGTON TIES

Nathan Beman was a seventeen-year-old from Shoreham, Vermont, near
Lake Champlain, when he was asked to guide Ethan Allen across the lake.
His family lived in Manchester in Bennington County, and he returned to
Manchester to marry a Manchester woman. He later moved to New York
and was one of the first founders of Chateaugay, New York, where he is
buried. His name is listed on the war memorial on the green across from
the Equinox Hotel in Manchester.

Noah Phelps, the spy, was from Connecticut, but he was with the group that
passed through Bennington County with the request to get Ethan Allen
and his Green Mountain Boys to lead an attack. It took real patriotism to
act as a lone spy, entering Fort Ticonderoga and gathering information—
all at the risk of discovery.

Captain Edward Mott from Preston, Connecticut, was elected chairman of the Council of War and supported Ethan Allen as field commander. Mott also produced a very good log of the expedition.

John Brown, the lawyer who came through Bennington from Massachusetts (Berkshires), would later lead successful raids on the British in Lake Champlain.

Colonel James Easton brought troops to Bennington from Pittsfield, Massachusetts, to support the expedition. He was elected second in command.

Colonel Seth Warner was third in command and led a raid just after the capture of Fort Ticonderoga to capture the small fort at Crown Point. This was America's second victory.

The *Roberts family*, with six participants (four from Manchester and two from Dorset) was the largest immediate family group on the expedition.

The extended *Allen family* had seven participants: Ethan's brothers Ira, Heman and Levi, plus cousins Seth Warner, Remember Baker and Ebenezer Allen.

Benedict Arnold is mentioned here only because he passed through Bennington County. After Lexington and Concord, Arnold had gone to the Council of Safety in Cambridge, Massachusetts, which authorized him to raise "400 men" in Western Massachusetts and lead an expedition to capture Fort Ticonderoga. Arnold, according to the Massachusetts Bicentennial Committee, on May 6 was in Williamstown, Massachusetts (about twelve miles south of Bennington). That same day, the Green Mountain Boys and the others were already on their way to Fort Ticonderoga. On May 8, Arnold traveled through Bennington County, stopping at Rupert. He wrote a letter asking for recruits. He caught up with Allen's group with no troops and only a manservant to help with his wardrobe. Responding to Arnold's claims that he should command the expedition because of the commission from Massachusetts, Edward Mott told him that him Ethan Allen was in command. Arnold persisted and went to Allen. There is no documentary evidence of the agreement between Allen and Arnold, but given that this disruption might have endangered the mission, Arnold was allowed to enter the fort as Ethan Allen's "left hand." There is no evidence that he in any way commanded the group. Even the author of a biography written in conjunction with the great-grandson of Benedict Arnold indicated that Arnold "was a volunteer," not the commander. Bull's diary also indicates that Arnold would be on the "left hand" of Ethan Allen upon entering the fort, but would not be in command.

It appears that the New York State Education Department, on its sign outside Fort Ticonderoga, has it right. Allen had both the men and their respect. Allen sent in spies and mustered the Green Mountain Boys. Allen sealed the roads to Fort Ticonderoga to keep the mission a secret. Allen ordered the boats that took them across Lake Champlain. Arnold did none of these things.

If other names are to be added to the expression "Ethan Allen and the Green Mountain Boys captured Fort Ticonderoga," individuals like Noah Phelps, Nathan Beman or some of the other Patriots involved should be added before Arnold. He did, in a small way, help in that he was an extra body, but there is no conclusive evidence that he was a commander or a co-commander.

THE AFTERMATH OF
THE CAPTURE

Following the capture of Fort Ticonderoga by Ethan Allen and the Green Mountain Boys, the fort was strengthened and a fortress was built across Lake Champlain (Mount Independence), allowing the fort to remain in American hands for over two years, until July 6, 1777. The cannons were taken in the winter of 1775–76 by Colonel Henry Knox to Boston and placed on Dorchester Heights, forcing the British to leave Boston and giving Washington his first major victory. Since 1901, March 17, the day the British left Boston, has been celebrated as Evacuation Day (it is also St. Patrick's Day) in some towns in the Boston area.

The morale of the colonists skyrocketed after what was essentially a group of farmers captured the "North American Gibraltar" of the British empire. Allen's capture of the fort was spectacular enough for the Continental Congress to authorize a formal Green Mountain Boy regiment. Representatives (not the Green Mountain Boys) from the Grants made Seth Warner head of this regiment. Ethan Allen later made an unauthorized attempt to capture Montreal and was captured. He spent about three years in prison in London and was released in 1778. He went on after his return to continue to fight for the United States and Vermont, and he died in 1789, before Vermont became the fourteenth state.

Remember Baker, Ethan Allen's cousin, was killed by natives during an attack on Canada. He was beheaded and buried in Canada. Seth Warner, after being appointed head of the Green Mountain Boys in 1775, achieved even greater glory in 1777, as will be seen later.

Benedict Arnold, in later years, was credited with military successes at Valcour Island, where he slowed a British armada moving up Lake Champlain, and at Saratoga, where he led a decisive victory in one of the engagements. He later became famous for trying to turn West Point over to the British.

So great an event was this first victory of the Revolution that two ships were designated *Ethan Allen*. The first was a wood ship in the 1860s. The second ship was the USS *Ethan Allen*, the first of the *Ethan Allen* class of nuclear submarines. It is interesting that one of the other four subs in the *Ethan Allen* class of submarines was the USS *Thomas Jefferson*. Thomas Jefferson, as secretary of state, visited the Walloomsac Inn, which was across the street from the Catamount Tavern in 1791 and almost directly across from where Ethan Allen lived in Bennington about fifteen years earlier. They had both walked on the same ground.

As a further tribute, the U.S. government issued a commemorative stamp in 1955 that depicted Fort Ticonderoga, a cannon and Ethan Allen.

The U.S. Route 7 was named the Ethan Allen highway in 1930. In Vermont, there was a dedication parade up the highway from the

USS *ETHAN ALLEN*
The first in the *Ethan Allen* class of nuclear submarines, it had sixteen missile tubes. It was in the film *The Hunt for Red October* and in 1962 it fired the only nuclear armed Polaris missile ever launched. Built at the Electric Boat Division of General Dynamics in Groton, Connecticut, the USS *Ethan Allen* was commissioned on August 8, 1961, and decommissioned on March 31, 1983. *U.S. government photo.*

1955 COMMEMORATIVE U.S.
POSTAGE STAMP
The stamp depicts Ethan Allen
and Fort Ticonderoga. Note
the size and layout of the fort
that Ethan Allen captured. *U.S.
government commemorative stamp.*

ETHAN ALLEN IV AND "PEGGY" LINCOLN BECKWITH, MANCHESTER
In 1930, Peggy Beckwith (Abraham Lincoln's great-granddaughter) flew over Ethan
Allen IV heading the parade dedicating Ethan Allen Highway (now Historic 7A).
Sections of the foundation of the hangar are still visible on the Hildene Meadowland.
Courtesy of Friends of Hildene, Inc.

Massachusetts line to Manchester (the same basic route taken by Ethan Allen and the Green Mountain Boys). As a tribute, Mary "Peggy" Lincoln Beckwith (the great-granddaughter of Abraham Lincoln) flew Ethan Allen IV over the parade route. Her biplane was based in Manchester at Hildene, which she later inherited.

A statue of Ethan Allen is permanently on view in Washington in Statuary Hall. As will be discussed in part three for his exploits in 1777 in Bennington County, the statue of another Patriot, John Stark, from New Hampshire is also with Ethan Allen in Statuary Hall.

1776

PRELUDE TO EVENTS OF 1777

In early 1776, Colonel Henry Knox delivered captured Fort Ticonderoga cannons to George Washington in Boston after an arduous two-month winter hike from the fort to the city.

The Americans beefed up their Fort Ticonderoga defenses and constructed Mount Independence across Lake Champlain from Fort Ticonderoga to control the narrows between the two forts on the lake. The British did try to invade from Canada via Lake Champlain, but they were forced to turn back before attacking the two forts.

On July 4, 1776, the United States declared its independence from Great Britain.

In Bennington County—Dorset to be precise—there were a series of conventions of representatives from various towns in the Grants. In the final convention held at the Cephas Kent Tavern on Dorset's West Road in September, delegates from many of the towns voted to form a "separate district" (state) from New York, New Hampshire and England. Again, the cause of the American Revolution and the cause of Vermont independence became even more closely tied. From this time on, the Green Mountain Boys would be dually fighting for the independence of the United States and the independence of the area that had been known as the Grants. New York, of course, did not recognize this vote and, in fact, would not recognize the independence of Vermont for another fifteen years. Tyler Resch, in his book *Dorset: In the Shadow of Marble Mountain*, offers a very good discussion of the Kent Tavern and Kent Inn.

1777

THE MARCH SOUTH TO THE BATTLE OF BENNINGTON:

Prelude to the Battle of Saratoga

THE BRITISH INVADE THE COLONIES FROM CANADA

Both Fort Ticonderoga and Mount Independence, on the eastern side of Lake Champlain, were still controlled by the colonists in the beginning of 1777. However, in England, British Lieutenant General John Burgoyne was presenting a plan to the Crown to end the war. He proposed that the British cut off New England from the rest of the colonies via a three-pronged attack. One army, under Burgoyne, would go down from Canada via Lake Champlain to Albany, New York, and on the way it would capture Fort Ticonderoga and regain control of the Champlain Valley. Another force, under Barry St. Leger, would go up the St. Lawrence River to Lake Ontario and then turn east down the Mohawk River to Albany. From the south, General Howe would lead a force up the Hudson River to Albany. With New England cut off and the Hudson River–Champlain Valley trade route in British hands, the British could then turn east and recapture cities like Boston.

Having received the approval from the Crown, Burgoyne arrived in Canada in the spring to make final preparations for his armada to invade Lake Champlain. His force was massive: he had assembled about thirty-seven hundred British forces, including some scouts, and about three thousand German mercenaries (from the Hesse-Hanau and Brunswick states in Germany), as well as Native American scouts. With artillery and other forces added, the total was over seven thousand. Including support personnel and women, the entire armada was approaching ten thousand people. As time went on, Burgoyne added to his forces with more Loyalist deserters and Native Americans and subtracted as he left some troops behind to guard the supply routes.

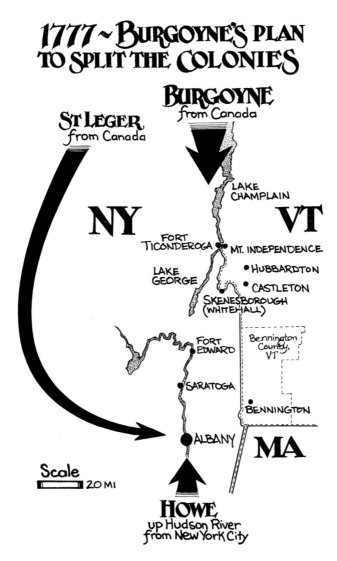

LIEUTENANT GENERAL JOHN BURGOYNE'S 1777 PLAN

Burgoyne planned to split the colonies with a three-pronged attack, resulting in the control of Lake Champlain and the Hudson River corridor. The plan did not succeed, and Burgoyne later said that Vermont had the "most active and rebellious people" on the continent.

MAJOR GENERAL ARTHUR ST. CLAIR
(CA. 1736–1818)
St. Clair evacuated Fort
Ticonderoga ahead of Burgoyne in
1777 and retreated south through
Dorset, Manchester, Sunderland
and Arlington and then to the Fort
Edward, New York area. He faced
a court martial for the evacuation,
but was cleared. Later, he became
president of the Continental
Congress. He crossed the Delaware
with George Washington prior to
the Battle of Trenton. *Courtesy of the
National Archives.*

ARTHUR ST CLAIR

By June 20, this armada was underway, heading south from Canada toward Fort Ticonderoga. In addition to the sheer numbers of Burgoyne's armada putting fear into the settlers in Vermont, Burgoyne made a proclamation on June 29 that would add to this fear and hopefully entice residents to go to the British side for protection. However, by using such words as "arbitrary imprisonment, confiscation of property, persecution and torture," many residents became even more determined to fight. And to make it even more repulsive, Burgoyne indicated that he intended to use Native Americans: "I have but to give stretch to the Indian Forces under my direction, and they amount to thousands." Many of the Bennington County Green Mountain Boys had fought in the French and Indian War and knew exactly what Burgoyne meant.

By July 3, the invaders were about three miles from the massive fortifications of Fort Ticonderoga and Mount Independence on Lake Champlain. Unfortunately, contrary to the impression of most people in New England and the rest of the colonies, these forts in 1777 were not as impregnable as they had been the prior year. Many of the recruits had gone home (the Continental army had many short-term enlistees). Both garrisons were commanded by American General Arthur St. Clair (born

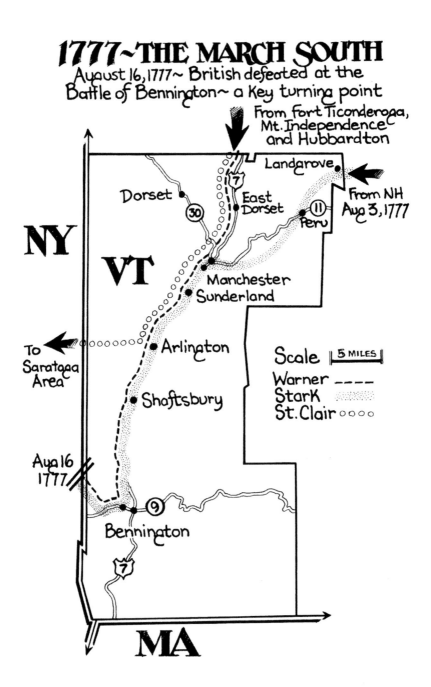

THE MARCH SOUTH

The map depicts the movement of troops south through Bennington County parallel to Burgoyne's movement south through the Champlain and Hudson Valleys. The result was the victory at the Battle of Bennington.

ca. 1736), but at this time his able-bodied troop strength was down from ten thousand to about twenty-five hundred, making it difficult to man two forts, the waterway, the outlying areas and, most importantly, the high hill behind the fort known as Sugar Loaf or Mount Defiance.

Burgoyne found out that Mount Defiance was not defended, and he was able to cut a short road through the woods and bring artillery up to the top undetected. On July 5, the Americans discovered the cannon on the top of Mount Defiance and realized that to try to defend the two forts was hopeless. St Clair and his officers made the decision to evacuate and save the army to fight again. In the middle of the night on July 6, the Americans in Fort Ticonderoga crossed the wooden floating bridge connecting Fort Ticonderoga and Mount Independence and, along with troops from the garrison at Mount Independence, took the road southeast toward Castleton. Some sick American defenders and other troops escaped by boat south to Skenesborough (Whitehall) at the southern tip of Lake Champlain.

The Americans were not able to burn the bridge across the lake, and a large body of British soldiers under General Fraser gave chase to the Americans into Vermont. In the early morning of July 7, the British caught up with the Americans at a Vermont town called Hubbardton— about twenty miles southeast of Fort Ticonderoga. The main body of General St. Clair's troops had already gone through Hubbardton and had left behind a smaller force of mainly Massachusetts and Vermont troops. The overall command of the Americans at Hubbardton was put upon Bennington County's Seth Warner. Colonel Ebanezer Francis (Massachusetts) was there, and though he fought valiantly with Warner, he was killed in the battle. As the British charged and overran the American positions at the end of the battle, Seth Warner shouted instructions to the Green Mountain Boys to disperse and meet in Manchester. Although technically losing the battle, these Patriots were able to hold off the well-trained and armed British forces long enough to allow St. Clair's main army to escape south intact. The battle at Hubbardton was later called one of the most successful rear guard actions in American military history. The Americans fought fiercely, causing the British to lose (dead and wounded) about 20 percent of the forces sent to Hubbardton.

The fall of Fort Ticonderoga and Mount Independence created major panic. The British (under Fraser) and the Germans (under General Riedesel) stayed for a couple of days on the battlefield (now a Vermont Historic Site) to care for the wounded and regroup, but then generally moved south to Castleton and west to Skenesborough. Most importantly, however, on July

10, Burgoyne—in a move that would have major impact on Bennington County—ordered Riedesel to march his five German regiments <u>back</u> to Castleton. This was a very deliberate move on Burgoyne's part to create the impression that there were armed forces in Vermont ready to invade Bennington County and the rest of New England to the south.

Meanwhile, Seth Warner and the remainder of the American forces from Hubbardton were working their way south to Manchester and would make Manchester their headquarters.

On July 5, the reinforced "Gibraltar" and another garrison on Mount Independence were blocking Burgoyne's march south. The next day, July 6, they had been abandoned without a shot being fired. All of New England and the path to New York City were open to the British army. The British were camped in Vermont on the Castleton River and no one knew their plans.

People were evacuating the northern Vermont towns and retreating south to Manchester and to points farther south like Bennington and the Berkshires for protection. The roads were "a scene of confusion." According to a Living History Association article:

> *the greater portion of the scattered inhabitants of Rutland County (just to the north of Bennington County), after the Battle of Hubbardton, sought safety in flight south to Manchester and Bennington.*

Some people even fled "leaving the fat boiling." In Poultney (a town Ethan Allen had helped defend against the New Yorkers), some residents were having a church service in a log building on July 8 when word reached them about Hubbardton. According to the *History of Poultney*, they all left at once, "not even visiting their homes," and made their way on foot to Bennington without stopping. Ira Allen summed it up by saying that because of this fear of the Germans and British moving south in Vermont,

> *near three quarters of the people on the west side of the Green Mountains were forced to remove.*

(Allen may have exaggerated, but it was no doubt a large number.) Some residents were so afraid that they decided to become Tories and seek the protection of the British.

To put this situation in perspective, the seventeen towns of today's Bennington County probably had, in 1777, a population of around three thousand. The combat regulars of the invading force totaled about seven thousand. Estimates (some exaggerated) were that three thousand to four thousand troops were already camped in Vermont at Castleton.

Geography helped to support the fear of the invasion of Bennington County. As long as Ticonderoga blocked Burgoyne's southern march and the British troops were on the west shore of Lake Champlain, there was no major immediate threat. Once, however, the British troops were in Vermont to the north (Castleton), thirty miles from Manchester, they could choose to go south via the Vermont Valley from Rutland to Dorset and Manchester or down via the Mettewee Valley into Dorset and then into Manchester. Once in Manchester, they could go south to Arlington and then west through the Batten Kill Valley toward Albany or continue south to Bennington and then west to Albany. They could also go to other parts of New England.

DESTINATION MANCHESTER

While Burgoyne was planning and then marching south down the Champlain Valley to the west, representatives from the towns of the Grants were holding a series of conventions in the neighboring towns of Westminster and Windsor on the Connecticut River to the east.

On January 15, Vermont had officially declared its independence and adopted the name "New Connecticut" for the proposed state. On July 6, it changed its name to "Vermont" as a contraction of the French words for "green" and "mountain." That same day, word reached the convention that Ticonderoga had been evacuated and the British were in Hubbardton. A rainstorm forced the delegates to stay to finish their work, so on July 8, they adopted the Vermont Constitution, formalizing the independent Vermont. The delegates also created a twelve-member Council of Safety to govern Vermont until elections could be held. The convention adjourned immediately and council members headed to Manchester—in the path of an invading army—to hold their first sessions of the new state. This new state was about 150 miles long from the Massachusetts line to the Canadian border in the north, yet in a few days, Manchester—thirty miles from the southern border—had become the northernmost relatively safe town.

St. Clair was also headed to Manchester. He had gone from Hubbarton to Castleton, but because the road south to the Hudson River ahead of Burgoyne was threatened by British troops to the west, he went east to

Rutland. On July 7, St. Clair wrote from Rutland that he would be going south to Bennington to get provisions and then west to the Hudson River. From Rutland, he moved south to the Bennington County town of Dorset (the next town north of Manchester), where he stayed at the house of William Marsh. Marsh was a big landowner in Dorset and Manchester and owned the Marsh Tavern in Manchester where the Council of Safety would meet. Although he was a rebel supporter on July 7, 1777, within one week he became a Tory as Burgoyne and his troops approached. He apparently wanted to protect his landholdings and thought that the British would win. In a letter from Dorset dated July 8, St. Clair wrote to General Schuyler, head of the northern army in the Hudson Valley, to indicate that if he could get provisions in Manchester, he would go directly to the Saratoga area via Arlington. He also indicated that Colonel Warner's regiment and the state militia should be left in Manchester to protect the state after he departed. According to Richard Ketchum in *Saratoga*, St. Clair, on July 9, was then in Manchester at the Marsh Tavern.

It is not known exactly how many of St. Clair's troops came through Bennington County, but it has been estimated that he left Ticonderoga with about twenty-five hundred. Since some troops were left as the rear guard at Hubbardton and some escaped down Lake Champlain, roughly a thousand to fifteen hundred may have actually come through the county. It is believed that St. Clair got the provisions he needed in Manchester and then took the most direct route to the Hudson Valley by going south through Sunderland to Arlington and west (about thirty miles) to the Fort Edward area, where he arrived on July 12.

THE COUNCIL OF SAFETY TAKES ACTION IN MANCHESTER

Having passed the Vermont constitution on July 8 at Windsor, the members of the Council of Safety went to Manchester. By July 11, in the midst of chaos and panic, the Council of Safety was already issuing correspondence. These first meetings in Manchester were held at the Marsh Tavern.

There is no list of the twelve Council of Safety members, but the top three members—Thomas Chittenden, president; Jonas Fay, vice-president; and Ira Allen, secretary—had strong ties in Bennington County. In addition, members Joseph Fay, Moses Robinson and Nathan Clark were also from Bennington County. This council faced the task of governing a new state with no money and a trained enemy army poised to invade from the north, only thirty miles away.

VERMONT ASKS FOR HELP FROM OTHER STATES

St. Clair's troops had passed through Manchester and the only troops remaining in Manchester were the remnants of Seth Warner's regiment from Hubbardton and some miscellaneous militia. Warner's troops, the only ones left to defend the new Vermont, were camped southwest about half a mile from the Marsh Tavern on what is now Historic Route 7A. Among the immediate actions taken in Manchester was a letter dated July 15 that Ira Allen, secretary of the Council of Safety,

MARSH TAVERN∘1769

THE MARSH TAVERN, MANCHESTER
Built in 1769, it was the origin of what became the Equinox Hotel. The Council of Safety of the new state of Vermont held its first sessions here in July 1777 and decided to seize Tory properties to support raising troops. This was the first time in U.S. history that this was done. The Green Mountain Boys also met here. From here, a letter was sent to New Hampshire asking for help, resulting in John Stark coming to Bennington. *Courtesy of Manchester Historical Society and William Badger.*

sent to New Hampshire, seeking immediate military help. This letter is presented in its entirety to show the desperate situation in Manchester and Vermont. Very cleverly, Ira Allen explained the domino effect—if Vermont fell, then New Hampshire would be left alone with an open frontier and Vermont couldn't help. Although probably exaggerated, his postscript gave a feel for the size of the army in Castleton. His letter (in part shown in its original style) was also sent to Massachusetts.

The Honorable Council of Safety of New Hampshire

In Council of Safety, State of Vermont
Manchester, 15th July 1777
Gentlemen:
This state in particular seems to be at Present the object of Distruction. By the surrender of the fortress Ticonderoga a communication is opened to the Defenceless inhabitants on the frontier. Who having little more in store than sufficient for the maintenance of their Respective families and not ability to immediately remove their effects are therefore induced to accept such Protections as are offered them by the Enemy; by this means Those Towns that are most Contiguous to them are under necessity of Taking such Protections by which the Town or Towns become equally a frontier as the former Towns before such protection, and unless we can obtain the assistance of our friends so as to put it immediately in our Power to make a sufficient stand against such strength as they may send, it appears that it will soon be out of power of this state to maintain a frontier.

This country, not withstanding its infancy, seems as well supplied with provisions for Victualing an army as any country on the continent so that on that account we cannot see why a stand may not as well be made in this State as in the State of New Hampshire and more especially as in the inhabitants are heartily disposed to Defend their Liberties.

You Gentlemen will at once sensible that every town such own as accepts protection are rendered at that instant forever incapable of affording us any further assistance, and what is infinitely worse, as some Disaffected persons eternally Lurk in almost every town such become Doubly fortified to injure their Country. Our Good Dispositions to defend ourselves and make a frontier for your state with our own cannot be carried into execution without your assistance.

Should you send immediate assistance we can help you and should you neglect till we are put to the necessity of taking protection you Readily Know it is in a moment out of our power to assist you. Laying these Circumstances together will I hope induce Your Honors to take the same into consideration and immediately send us your Determination in the Premises.

I have the satisfaction to be your Honors' most Obedient
and very humble servant

Ira Allen, Secr;y

P.S. By express this moment received we learn that between
<u>*three and four thousand of the Enemy*</u> *are fortifying at the*
town of Castleton. Our Case calls for immediate assistance.

From Manchester on July 15, another letter was sent to "All Militia Officers whom it may concern" and was signed by Ira Allen. In this letter, he also asked for help, but more specifically, he called for the defense of Manchester. Ira Allen's letters made the following very specific observation about the British and German movements: "The Continental Stores at Bennington seem to be their present aim."

VERMONT DECIDES TO FINANCE ITS OWN MILITIA BY SEIZING TORY PROPERTY

Before the Council of Safety adjourned south to Bennington, this group took another important action. Sending letters to request help was one way to get forces into town to defend the new state, but forces had to be raised by Vermont itself. Unfortunately, troops cost money—they required clothing, food, etc. At first, it was thought that only two companies (of sixty men each) could be raised, but Ira Allen thought Vermont would need many more troops. Since it was he who suggested increasing the numbers, the task of finding a way to pay for them became his. Living up to the task, Allen—in his own later writings—indicated that the next morning he would announce his plan to raise money to pay for these troops. The plan he announced was simple: the Council of Safety should appoint commissioners of sequestration with the ability to take the property of Tories and sell it to raise money for the state to fund the militia.

This concept today would be unheard of—and it was unheard of then. In fact, Ira Allen later stated, "This was the first instance in America of seizing and selling the property of the enemies of American independence." (As a side note, four months later, on November 27, 1777, the Continental Congress recommended that all the colonies should take the same action.)

It is also ironic that one of the first properties in the United States to be confiscated was in Manchester, and it turns out that it was William Marsh's properties. Marsh, less than a week before, had met with the head of the American army, St. Clair, in Dorset. At that time, he had been a Patriot. Marsh left for Canada and was later permitted back to live in Dorset. He died in Dorset and is buried in the East Dorset cemetery.

So confident of their ability to raise money for troops, the Council of Safety almost immediately appointed Samuel Herrick to be lieutenant colonel of a new organization: the Green Mountain Rangers. Herrick, who had come to Bennington in 1768, was well qualified, given that he had been a Green Mountain Boy captain in Ethan Allen's militia and he had been with Ethan Allen at the capture of Fort Ticonderoga. Herrick made his headquarters in Manchester "adjacent" to Colonel Warner's Continental regiment. One of the captains of a company of Green Mountain Rangers was John Warner, brother of Seth Warner. Moving quickly on July 18, Herrick ordered Ebenezer Allen (distant cousin of Ethan Allen) north with his company to scout Riedesel's position in the Castleton area.

A Different Manchester in 1777

The Manchester that was the host in 1777 to the Council of Safety meetings and the troops of Warner and Herrick was different than the Manchester of two years before, when the Green Mountain Boys passed through on their way to capturing Fort Ticonderoga in 1775. Changing loyalties were the main difference. Many of the larger landowners in Manchester tended to think they could preserve their holdings if they sided with the British. They risked everything if they sided with the rebels and the British won. It was amazing what an overwhelming force of about seven thousand troops thirty miles away did to the loyalties of some people in a town of roughly a thousand.

In addition to William Marsh, another notable example of switching loyalties was Jeremiah French. (William Marsh had married his daughter.) French had vast landholdings in Manchester, and both of his former homes still stand on Manchester's Main Street. One is about three quarters of a mile south of Manchester Village (Manchester itself in 1777). French actually fled Manchester. He joined the Queen's Loyal Rangers on July 5 (the day before Fort Ticonderoga fell to Burgoyne) and later was taken prisoner at the Battle of Bennington on August 16, 1777. He had left Bennington County in July as a large landowner and returned to Bennington County in August as a prisoner. He was in a prisoner exchange and eventually died in Canada as a respected citizen.

JEREMIAH FRENCH HOUSE, MANCHESTER.
Jeremiah French, who was one of the original settlers of Manchester, built the house at least as early as 1774. His daughter married William Marsh, who owned the Marsh Tavern. It has a beautiful preserved "hip roof" design. It is now a private residence.

Jeremiah also had another house, which was across the street from the Marsh Tavern. It is now known as the 1811 House. This house was actually built around 1770, but was converted to an inn in 1811—hence the name. Over a hundred years later, that house was to be occupied by Mary Lincoln Isham (Abraham Lincoln's granddaughter), who would eventually inherit the Lincoln family home, Hildene, in Manchester.

At the same time, Manchester was producing some of the most fervent rebels. Gideon Ormsby was a captain in the Green Mountain Boys. (His name is inscribed on the war memorial in Manchester Village that, ironically, stands between the former Tory properties of William Marsh and Jeremiah French). Ormsby was so fervent and respected as a Revolutionary War soldier that Edward Isham—the law partner of Abraham Lincoln's son, Robert Todd Lincoln—renamed Purdy's Hill to Ormsby Hill. The Isham home is now the historic Inn at Ormsby Hill. Other Manchester notables were the Roberts family members—"the fighting Roberts family"—with four members in Manchester and two in Dorset. Not only were they with Ethan Allen at Ticonderoga, but at least three (Peter, John Jr. and Benjamin) also joined the force that would move south to Bennington.

NEW HAMPSHIRE'S JOHN STARK COMES TO BENNINGTON COUNTY TO HELP
With One Condition

After receiving the calls for help from Vermont, New Hampshire wasted no time. It almost immediately agreed to send troops to help Vermont, and its choice for a commander was unanimous: John Stark. His credentials were solid. He had gone into retirement after being passed over for a promotion, but he was a New Englander. He had proven himself at the Battle of Bunker Hill (Breeds Hill) and during the French and Indian Wars. He was a Patriot and a leader. Stark, who was born in 1728 in New Hampshire, agreed to command the men under one condition: that his command be independent, reporting to the New Hampshire legislature and not, if he chose, to the Continental army. New Hampshire agreed.

The New Hampshire legislature sent a letter of confirmation to Brigadier General John Stark, clearly indicating his independent command. (Shown in older style. Underline is the author's.)

> *July 19, 1777*
>
> *You are hereby required to repair to Charlestown, No 4, so as to be there by the 24ᵗʰ—Thursday next, to meet and confer with persons appointed by the Convention of the State of Vermont relative to the route of the troops under your command, their being supplied with provisions, and future operations, and when the troops are collected at No. 4 you are to take the Command of them and march them into the State of Vermont. And there act in conjunction with the troops of that state or any other state or of the United States, or separately, as it shall appear Expediant to you for the protection of the people or the annoyance of the enemy and from time to time as occasion shall require said Intelligence to the General Assembly of Committee of Safety of your operations and the maneuvers of the enemy.*
>
> *M. Weare*
> *(President of the State of New Hampshire)*

Almost immediately, the charismatic Stark started mustering volunteers at the fort at No. 4. (Charlestown, New Hampshire—just across the Connecticut River from Vermont—was called at the time "No. 4" and was about twenty miles north of Brattleboro, Vermont.) Stark's similarities to Ethan Allen are obvious in the sense that both had charisma and men would serve under them with very little question. Stark was assembling a force of farmers that had almost no uniforms, no tents, few bayonets, only one mold to make bullets and probably only one old cannon (unmounted at that). To get lead for ammunition, some soldiers brought in clock weights, pewter spoons and porringers to be melted.

As troops became ready, Stark sent them off in groups of about a hundred to Manchester. He eventually had over twelve hundred militia from New Hampshire heading to the Vermont frontier. Stark left New Hampshire on August 3 and chose the general route suggested by Ira Allen via Chester. (By the time Stark's odyssey was finished, he would have been in ten of the seventeen towns in current-day Bennington County.)

Stark's first entry into today's Bennington County was in Landgrove, even today a bucolic little town. The Utley family, who actually thought they were in Peru to the west, originally settled it. However, it was eventually discovered that the Peru line ended and Weston didn't begin for a mile or so to the east. The Utleys were actually in ungranted space, but they did later (in 1780) petition Vermont to charter Landgrove as a town.

Town records indicate that Stark's troops entered Landgrove from the east over what is now Old County Road, which was the first road into the area from the Connecticut River area. This road drops down and then crosses Landgrove Road to what is now Hapgood Pond Road. Hapgood Pond Road then crosses Utley Flats to the place where Captain William Utley had a farm and some troops stopped to eat. The flats, a stream and the farm area are still visible today. The farm has undergone many changes to its original appearance. It is said that Captain Utley died on the farm and is buried there, but excavations have not been able to find his remains.

From Captain Utley's, there was no "road" west to Peru, so the troops then had to cut a five- to six-mile road west to what is now the village of Peru. This road was cut parallel to and a little north of what is now Hapgood Pond Road and probably passed through what is now Hapgood Pond (a man-made recreation area today). This route would have brought them to what is today North Road, which then meets Hapgood Pond Road. Since they probably had an unmounted cannon, they needed to make a path wide enough to allow passage of the cannon. Whitelaw's 1796 map shows that even twenty years after 1777, there was still only one road from Landgrove and it is shown passing near Hapgood Pond.

Although the troops left New Hampshire over a period of several days, they may have camped more than one night in Peru. Various sources indicate that Stark himself was in Peru on August 6. A monument (small obelisk) was later placed by the Sons and Daughters of Vermont to show the location of the encampment of Stark's troops. There is a spring nearby. Given the number of troops involved, the encampment may have been spread out. There is indication that some troops went a little farther in Peru and camped near where General Dudley later had a house just past Peru Village. The monument in Peru is about three hundred yards from the village of Peru. (If you can't visit the area, the film *Baby Boom* with Diane Keaton has a view of Peru from above and also a short shot of her driving across Utley Flats in Landgrove.)

From Peru, Stark went on to Manchester and arrived on August 7. The route taken from Peru to Manchester was probably not the current Route 11. Carl Chapin, in a publication by the Manchester Historical Society, indicates that Stark went across the valley (French Hollow) and then up and over the Green Mountains at Downer Glen, which is where Bourne Brook drops down into Manchester. Older maps seem to indicate that there was at least a path down Bourne Brook. Some of Stark's troops then apparently crossed the Vermont Valley and went up the foothills of the Taconic Mountains to camp in Manchester near the Yester House, which is now part of the Southern Vermont Arts Center (SVAC). There were natural springs nearby. Not all troops may have taken this route. Some may have come down by Bromley Brook a little north of the current Route 11.

BURGOYNE'S SLOW MOVE SOUTH AND HIS TACTICAL ERROR

Meanwhile, from the capture of Fort Ticonderoga in July until August 7, when Stark arrived in Manchester, Burgoyne had been moving his main force south toward Albany from Skenesborough (Whitehall) at the southern end of Lake Champlain. He then made a tremendous tactical error. He could have gone back to Fort Ticonderoga and taken a three-mile portage to Lake George. At the southern end of Lake George, he could have taken a well-used five-mile portage to the Hudson River. Instead, Burgoyne chose to build a twenty-three-mile road south from Skenesborough through swamps and forest to the Hudson River.

Besides the obstacles of the swamps and the forest, the Americans were using very effective weapons—farm implements like the axe—to delay his march. Trees were cut and branches were interlocked on the small Wood Creek to make it difficult to move supplies south. Swamps were also flooded. Burgoyne's army, now totaling about six thousand troops, slowed to a crawl. It took him about twenty-four days to go twenty-three miles. His expedition at times stretched for over three miles. As Burgoyne moved south, his supply lines were becoming long and he was using up supplies. Horses to pull carriages and to mount his Hessians/Brunswickers were simply not available. Around July 30, Burgoyne finally reached the Hudson River.

THE SITUATION IN BENNINGTON COUNTY

August 7, 1777

By August 7, Riedesel and his German forces had moved back from Castleton to join Burgoyne's main army on the Hudson River to the west of Manchester. This had relieved a little pressure from the threat of an invasion directly south into Bennington County from Castleton in the north. However, there was still the possibility of passing through the Taconic Mountains from the west via the Batten Kill Valley in Arlington or south at Bennington. In particular, the majestic thirty-eight-hundred-foot-high Mount Equinox—the tallest mountain in the Taconic range—west of Manchester offered some protection, but there were still many gaps through which the troops could move.

Not only could an army invade the Vermont Valley, but there were also reasons known to both sides for Burgoyne's army to invade. Burgoyne was running low on supplies and Bennington County had what he needed. Cattle were being driven from points north to join other cattle in Bennington County, then were moved south from Manchester to Bennington and west to the markets in Albany and New York and then, as Burgoyne said later, to "the main army" of the rebels.

The town of Bennington itself had become attractive for supplies and therefore might become attractive to the British. Bennington was on a north–south corridor starting on the western side of the Green Mountains and going south into Massachusetts. It was also located on an east–west corridor from New Hampshire and Boston through Brattleboro along the southern end of Vermont, into Bennington County and Bennington and then on to Albany. Historically, intersections of roads became attractive places to have supply depots or distribution facilities. Also, there was a hill near the Catamount Tavern with grazing areas that could be used. Bennington was situated on Burgoyne's left flank and not directly in his path if he continued along the Hudson River Valley. In short, Bennington did become a storehouse for military supplies.

To help improve the storage of supplies in Bennington, a man named Isaac Tichenor came to Bennington around June 14, 1777, as an assistant to the commissary general to buy supplies for the Northern Department of the Continental army. These supplies would become an increasingly tempting target for the British. Tichenor had been operating out of Williamstown and was familiar with Bennington. He was a Princeton graduate and had been called "Jersey Slick." (Jersey Slick would eventually build a house [still in existence] in Bennington, within walking distance of the Catamount Tavern, and become a five-time governor of Vermont.) There was also a system that encouraged the rapid buildup of supplies for the Continental army. Agents were paid a commission on what they could buy. Hence, the more you bought, the bigger the commission.

It was reported that on August 6, Burgoyne wrote in his orderly book: "Sixth August. At ten o'clock this morning, not quite enough provisions for the consumption of two days." Vermont didn't know how bad the situation was for Burgoyne, but Stark was guessing correctly that the British were short on supplies. Vermont had these supplies, and there were ways for Burgoyne to get into the Vermont Valley to retrieve them.

By August 7, the Council of Safety had moved from Manchester to Bennington via Sunderland, Arlington and Shaftsbury. Early council letters indicate that it was actually in session in Bennington as early as July 28. The council itself only needed a quorum of its twelve members to be in session. Minutes of these meetings are not available, but a small group of seven or so could have met almost anywhere along the route to Bennington.

THE AUGUST 7 MANCHESTER CONFRONTATION
General Lincoln and General Stark

To help in the defense against Burgoyne's massive army moving south from Fort Ticonderoga, George Washington sent a new general to help— Lieutenant General Benjamin Lincoln (born 1733). Although somewhat overweight, he was still capable and, most of all, he was a New Englander

GENERAL BENJAMIN LINCOLN (1733–1810)
Lincoln was a "citizen-farmer" from Massachusetts. He later became secretary of war (1781–1783), Washington's second in command at Yorktown. Lincoln, Vermont, is named after him. *Courtesy of National Archives.*

from Massachusetts. General Schuyler, who was head of the Northern Army responsible for stopping Burgoyne's march south, sent Lincoln to Manchester.

When Stark arrived in Manchester on August 7, he found that some of his troops were preparing, at Lincoln's request, to go to the Hudson River to help Schuyler against Burgoyne. Massachusetts had also sent Cushing's Worcester County militia. However, when Stark and Lincoln met, Stark made it clear that his troops were not leaving Vermont, but were going south to Bennington. Stark would not follow the orders of the general of the Northern Army. Stark, in very blunt but reasoned words, said that his was an independent command—he could make decisions on whom to serve, but he was responsible to the New Hampshire legislature, not the Continental army. Stark's desire was to protect Vermont as the frontier to New Hampshire. Some Massachusetts troops were obligated to move to the Saratoga area. Schuyler was upset, but Lincoln—to his credit—was reasonable.

Stark, in his rationalization and to soften the refusal, indicated that even George Washington thought it was, in general, good to have an army on the flank of an advancing army to harass them. At Bennington, he could protect the supplies he was sure the British would come after directly, and at the same time he would be in a position to help harass Burgoyne's left flank. Stark's decision to protect Bennington would be momentous in the months and years to come. Lincoln realized that he couldn't change Stark's mind and decided to work with him, promising to try to convince Schuyler of the wisdom of Stark's plan.

THE ACTION MOVES SOUTH
TO BENNINGTON

Stark left Manchester for Bennington on August 8. Colonel Seth Warner also went to Bennington, although some of Warner's troops remained in Manchester under Lieutenant Colonel Samuel Safford (of Bennington) to provide some protection for Manchester. Stark and his troops traveled south from Manchester on the Route Historic 7A corridor in the Vermont Valley. Some accounts have Stark arriving in Bennington on the ninth and some have him arriving on the tenth, but there is evidence that Stark's camp was in Bennington on the ninth so it is likely that he arrived that day. We are blessed with a diary from one of Stark's soldiers, John Wallace, who indicated that he (Wallace) arrived in Manchester on August 7, stayed in Manchester two days and then marched to Shaftsbury on the tenth. On Monday, August 11, he went on to Bennington. We don't know exactly where Stark was on the night of August 8, but if he stayed along the route for a night, it would be consistent with claims that troops stayed in Shaftsbury before going to Bennington. The Wallace diary also helps confirm that leaders such as Stark did not always travel with their troops.

Shaftsbury (the last town before Bennington) was a stopping point (Galusha's Inn) for the expedition going north to capture Fort Ticonderoga, and it has a rich Revolutionary War history. Shaftsbury itself provided the Galusha brothers—David and Jonas—who would fight later in the Battle of Bennington. Jonas would be present at the surrender of Burgoyne and later became a nine-term governor of Vermont. There are also references in the book *Ordinary Heroes* that Seth Warner camped near the Waldo Tavern prior to the Battle of Bennington and prayers were held there during that period. The National Register of Historic Places indicates that the Waldo Barn may have been built in 1767, and local lore claimed that Seth Warner and his men used the stable for their "remounts" prior to the Battle of Bennington. This stable site is behind the White Column house in the Shaftsbury Historic District. Some of Warner's men were still in Manchester, so it was not a full regiment in Shaftsbury. Warner's troops were also apparently fed at the Waldo Tavern. There is some logic to this activity in the area, given that David Galusha—whose inn was within walking distance north about a few hundred feet—was a captain with Seth Warner's Green Mountain Boys. Jonas Galusha had also just been with Seth Warner at the Battle of Hubbardton.

The Abiathar and Rachael Waldo House (circa 1765) was used to store meat during the Revolution, as indicated by early meat hooks found in the basement. The National Register says that a 1780 Freeman's meeting indicated that meat should be stored in "Waldo's house" and flour and grain at "Captain Galusha's, innkeeper." Galusha's Inn was, and still is, near the Waldo house. Later in the Revolution, storage of supplies became a requirement, but it is possible that storage of meat was occurring in 1777.

Shaftsbury had munitions supplies as well. A munitions storage facility was just east of Historic 7A in South Shaftsbury, about a hundred yards on Buck Hill Road. The house, built in 1770, had some fortresslike features. That house, with some attractive renovations, is visible and discernable today. Farther south on Historic 7A was a house built in 1769 that would have been seen by any troops passing by. It is now the Robert Frost Museum, since Frost lived there in the early 1900s.

Settlers fleeing Burgoyne's army south from Manchester to Bennington would have gone through Shaftsbury. Given the many references and the many buildings known to be existing in August 1777, it would appear that most of the travelers going south in July and August of 1777 went down what is the Route 7A corridor today. Although there might been a north–south road to the east (East Road), it is not known when houses such as the Topping Tavern were built or the extent of development of the road itself in August 1777.

Why did Shaftsbury play such a major role? The original ejection trials with Ethan Allen involved Shaftsbury, so the Green Mountain Boys had been in town frequently. Additionally, Shaftsbury's location as the first town north of Bennington meant that it was heavily traveled. Also, as

MUNITIONS HOUSE, SHAFTSBURY
This home was used to store munitions during the Revolutionary War, including during the Battle of Bennington. It exists today after renovations as a private house. *Courtesy of Vermont Historical Society.*

indicated today, its beautiful rolling farmland along Historic 7A made it very favorable for a stopover or to obtain supplies. (In addition, as will be described later, the western section of Shaftsbury was part of the Bennington Battle theater.) In 1775, Shaftsbury actually had more people than Bennington and was only about fifteen miles from Manchester.

In Bennington, Stark made his headquarters initially at the Catamount Tavern (see image on page 26). The council room in the Catamount Tavern was active, as was the town itself. With refugees coming down

DIMMICK'S TAVERN (STAND), BENNINGTON
Colonel Samuel Herrick's former home, General Stark's troops camped here from August
9 to August 13, 1777, before moving north to another camp in North Bennington. Herrick
was a hero of the Battle of Bennington. A marker erected by New Hampshire marks the
spot on current Route 9 West. *Courtesy of Vermont Historical Society.*

from the north, scouts being sent out daily and militia coming in daily,
Bennington was a bustling village those first few weeks of August 1777.

Stark's camp was established in Bennington about two miles west of
the Catamount Tavern on what is now Route 9. The camp was at what
is commonly referred to as Dimmick's Stand (Tavern)—which had been
Samuel Herrick's homestead (he lived there with his wife, Silence)—in the
shadow of Mount Anthony. Herrick had been appointed three weeks prior in
Manchester as head of a Green Mountain Ranger group. Stark was savvy to
capitalize on both Herrick's and Warner's knowledge of Bennington.

Many of the well-known Bennington leaders were also joining the
defensive forces: Elijah Dewey owner of the Walloomsac Inn across the
street from the Catamount and the son of the Pastor Jedediah Dewey,
who lived a few houses down; Stephen Fay, who owned the Catamount
Tavern, and his five sons, including Dr. Jonas Fay; and Aaron Hubbell.

While in Bennington, Isaac Tichenor—who had been appointed as
assistant commissary—became friends with Seth Warner. Just before the
battle, around August 12 or 13, Tichenor asked Stark for guards to take a
drove of cattle to Albany. Stark refused, but Warner provided fifty guards.
Tichenor would return to Bennington late in the day on August 16 after
taking the cattle to Albany.

Stark Was Right

Bennington was the Target

Burgoyne had indeed decided to get supplies in Vermont, and he selected a commander for a foraging party. The commander was a Lieutenant Colonel Friedrich Baum (some documents show the spelling as Baume). Although respected, he had never really had fighting experience, and his other big drawback was that he could not speak English. His mostly German force of about six hundred (estimates vary widely) also consisted of Native Americans, Loyalists and British.

Initial instructions from Burgoyne to Frederich Baum did not include going to Bennington. Extracts (partly in their original style) from Burgoyne's written instructions to the expedition leader Baum are shown below:

> *Instructions for Lt. Col. Baum:*
> *Headquarters, August 9, 1777*
> *The object of your Expedition is to try the Affections of the Country, to disconcert the Councils of the Enemy, to mount the Riedesel's Dragoons, to compleat Peters Corp, and to obtain large Supplies of Cattle, Horses, and Carriages.*
> *…[Y]ou are to proceed from Batten Kill to Arlington and take post there till the detachment of the Provincials under the command of Captain Sherwood shall join you from the southward. You are then to proceed to Manchester, where you will take post so as to secure the pass of the mountains on the*

road from Manchester to Rockingham; from hence you will detach Indians and light troops to the northward, toward Otter Creek. On their return and also receiving intelligence that no enemy is in force upon the Connecticut River you will proceed by the road over the mountains to Rockingham where you will take post. This will be the most distant part on the expedition… and you are afterwards to descend to Brattlebury and from that place by the quickest march you are to return by the great road to Albany…your detachments are to have orders to bring in to you all horses fit to mount the dragoons under your command or to serve as bat horses to the troops together with as many saddles and bridles as can be found. The number of horses requiste, besides those necessary for mounting the regiment of dragoons, ought to be 1300. If you can bring more for the use of the army it will be so much the better. Your parties are likewise to bring in wagons, and other convenient carriages with as many draft oxen as will be necessary to draw them and all cattle fit for slaughter (milch cows excepted) which are to be left for the use of inhabitants.

This initial foraging expedition of over a hundred miles was to include Arlington and Manchester, but there was no mention of Bennington. Instead of ammunition, the main objective was to be livestock: horses, oxen and cattle. The quantity of horses mentioned appears large—thirteen hundred for an army of around five to six thousand. Burgoyne seemed to be low on both draft horses and horses to mount his dragoons.

Bennington became the direct target when Burgoyne's scouts gave reports of the substantial supplies there. One account had a messenger from the Tory scout Captain Sherwood coming with news that there was a large rebel supply depot in a Vermont town guarded only by some four hundred local militia.

Baum's foraging party had actually started out with the intent of executing the original plan of entering Vermont at Arlington and then going to Manchester, but at 4:00 a.m. Burgoyne verbally ordered Baum to go directly to Bennington from Cambridge instead of going to Arlington. Baum was basically to avoid conflict and let Burgoyne know what to do if he encountered trouble.

Baum moved toward Bennington and skirmished with a very small group of Americans in Cambridge, New York, on August 13. Having

Stark was Right: Bennington was the Target

The Old Harmon Inn, 1770-1913.

THE HARMON INN, BENNINGTON
Built around 1769, the inn fell down in 1905. General Stark reportedly ate here on
August 14, 1777, before the Battle of Bennington. A marker now indicates the spot of
the inn. *Courtesy of Vermont Historical Society.*

SETH WARNER HOME, BENNINGTON
A few feet in front of the closest building is where Seth Warner lived while a resident
of Bennington during events of 1775–77. There is a marker indicating where the home
was located. The home was of similar design to the Henry House down the street.
Courtesy of Vermont Historical Society.

heard of the activity west of Bennington, after five days at Dimmick's Tavern, Stark, on the morning of fourteenth, moved his troops past the Harmon Inn (where it is reported that Stark had breakfast on the morning of August 14) and beyond the Breckenridge Farm, where there had been confrontations between the Green Mountain Boys and New Yorkers. Then the troops went near Seth Warner's house and crossed the Walloomsac River to a spot on the west side of Bennington, but on the east side of the meandering Walloomsac.

On the morning of August 14, Baum engaged a group of about two hundred troops headed by Colonel William Gregg, who had come out from Bennington to investigate after the first skirmish. He broke off the engagement and fell back, as did Stark, who had also been moving. Stark ended up camping on Harrington Road in Bennington, waiting for reinforcements. Baum was in a defensive position, also waiting for reinforcements, and Stark did not, at that time, want to attack a foe who was digging in.

Because of heavy rain, nothing significant happened in the battle theater on August 15, except word reached the Green Mountain Boys in Seth Warner's regiment (at the time under the command of Bennington's Samuel Safford) in Manchester that reinforcements were needed. They broke camp and marched south about twenty miles in the rain, arriving late. Indications are that they stopped to refresh near Harwood Hill in Bennington by some orchards, about a mile north from the Catamount Tavern. The current route Historic 7A is called, in the Bennington section, Harwood Hill Road, and there are still orchards in the area today.

The long night of the fifteenth and early on the sixteenth seemed beneficial to Stark. He had been reinforced first by more Vermont militia. Almost all the able-bodied men in Bennington were now available to fight. A party of militia from Massachusetts joined Stark. Included in this group was Reverend Thomas Allen—the fighting preacher—who demanded to fight or he would leave. Colonel Simonds (also spelled with a "y") was head of the Massachusetts group.

Stark, even without reinforcements, had found himself at the head of maybe 1,800 to 2,000 men on the morning of August 16, but accounts of the actual number vary widely. For instance, it is unknown how many Stockbridge Native Americans had come to help. Over 1,000 of the troops were from New Hampshire. Stark was not going to wait for reinforcements—he was going to attack. He had devised a magnificent plan involving a multipronged attack with reserves. Lieutenant Colonel Moses Nichols (New Hampshire), with at least 250 men, was going to cross into the southwest corner of Shaftsbury

(Bennington County) on his route around Baum and then move in behind Baum's left wing. Part of the plan to get behind the enemy was to look like Tories coming to help. The second group of about 300 to 350 men was made up of Vermonters, commanded by Colonels Herrick and Brush of Bennington, and they would go to the left around Baum's right wing. Colonels David Hobart and Thomas Stickney (New Hampshire), with about 200 men, were to go to the front to attack Tory positions. The fourth contingent of about 100 men was to go to the front to deceive and "amuse" the enemy. Stark's main body was to be held back in part, also to deceive the enemy. Also included were Colonel Williams from Wilmington and maybe forty New Yorkers. The low number from New York is understandable given that Burgoyne was heading down the Hudson Valley in New York at the same time.

THE BATTLE OF BENNINGTON BEGINS

Stark's headquarters had been off and on at the Catamount Tavern, where he had been consulting other leaders. Tradition says that Stark got up in the morning of August 16 and, seeing there was no rain, mounted his horse in front of the Catamount Tavern and road off to his camp for battle. Just before the battle, at his North Bennington camp, Stark made an inspirational speech. There have been several versions, but a common version is: "There are the red coats, and they are ours or this night Molly Stark sleeps a widow."

The multipronged attack plan was put into effect around noon. A monument marks the camp disembarkation point on Harrington Road in Bennington. The hills of New York can be seen from this monument and the direction of the routes can be observed. The men headed west

STARK'S CAMPSITE AUGUST 14–16, BENNINGTON
Stark camped here for three days during the Battle of Bennington. The hills in the distance to the left are New York, near where most of the action took place. Stark made his "Molly Stark" speech near here. From here, he sent Herrick and Brush off to the left and Nichols to the right to encircle the encamped British (Germans).

for Bennington Heights (as indicated on the map of Dunford) along the Walloomsac River, each via a different route.

At 3:00 p.m. the attack began. Baum was surrounded. It was an amazing battle, with untrained farmers without bayonets charging professionally trained British and German troops supported by four cannons using grapeshot. The next two hours, as Stark described it, were a "continual clap of thunder."

By 5:00 p.m. it was over—or so the troops thought. Troops had scattered to inspect the extensive battlefield and gather prisoners. Of course, in true New England fashion, they apparently opened a hogshead of rum to celebrate. But word reached Stark of German reinforcements. These reinforcements, under Colonel Breymann, had taken a long time to get to the battle area, but they were only a few miles west at 4:30 p.m. Stark tried to regroup his forces, but he was being forced back by Breymann with his two cannons and fresh troops.

Just when it seemed like there was going to be defeat after victory, Seth Warner's reinforcements from Manchester appeared. They had been at Harwood Hill ("about one mile north of Bennington"), then had marched to the village to get ammunition and were now arriving on the scene. The author Howard Coffin, in his book *Guns Over the Lake Champlain Valley*, described the scene: "As if scripted for an old Western movie in which the cavalry rides over the hill," Seth Warner and the Green Mountains Boys arrived to save the day. The German reinforcements were beaten back about a mile on what is now Route 67 (there is a monument at the site). As Stark wrote later, "Had sunlight lasted another hour we would have beat them all."

This description of the battle is brief. It is suggested that the reader who becomes interested in the battle pursue some of the more detailed accounts in the books mentioned in the bibliography or explore the area with some of the suggested tours. A very detailed and extensive book on the battle itself is *War Over the Walloomscoik* by Philip Lord.

RESOUNDING AMERICAN VICTORY
August 16, 1777

The Battle of Bennington was an overwhelming American victory. Of the thousand to twelve hundred British forces who marched to Bennington, seven hundred were taken prisoners, two hundred were killed and more were wounded. The German leader, Baum, and the Tory leader, Pfister—

both mortally wounded—were taken about two miles east from the spot they were wounded to a house in Shaftsbury, where they died within a day or so. Four cannons, a thousand rounds of ammunition, horses and drums were captured and taken to Bennington. (One cannon is now on display at the Bennington Museum, another is at the statehouse in Montpelier and the third is in New Hampshire.) The American losses were slight—about thirty dead and forty wounded out of the eighteen hundred to two thousand Americans in the battle. George Washington referred to the battle as "the great stroke struck by General Stark near Bennington."

The prisoners were marched to downtown Bennington. One of the guards was twenty-year-old Aaron Hubbell, who lived a mile west of Old Bennington and is now buried in the Old Cemetery. On the way back to the Catamount Tavern, many of the Bennington homes provided bread to the soldiers.

But there was even more shooting to come. The prisoners were mainly placed in the nearby old meetinghouse in Bennington, but some of the officers were placed in the Catamount Tavern across the street. Food was supplied in part by the Walloomsac Inn. The old meetinghouse also acted as a hospital. Speculation is that some tents or cloth from the storehouse

HOUSE WHERE BAUM DIED, SHAFTSBURY
Colonel Friedrich Baum, leader of the British forces (mainly German) that attacked Bennington, and Colonel Pfister (Tory leader) died in this house two days after the battle. The house was on Route 67 in Shaftsbury, about two miles from where he was wounded. The site is now indicated by a granite marker. *Courtesy of Vermont Historical Society.*

were used for a makeshift "hospital." During the day, a skirmish erupted between the prisoners and the colonists. The meetinghouse and the general area of the Walloomsac Inn was not equipped to handle the sudden influx of seven hundred prisoners, so there must have been crowding and shoving. Thinking some prisoners were trying to escape, some guards apparently fired on them—three prisoners died. Those Germans and Americans who died were put together in a mass grave in the Old Burying Ground (Old Cemetery) across the green from the old meetinghouse and behind Ethan Allen's former home.

The image on the cover of this book portrays the scene in Old Bennington with the prisoners. Colonels Herrick and Warner are shown on the back cover with John Stark featured with a sword on the front cover. Although a variety of the uniforms are shown, many of the participants on the colonists' side did not have uniforms. As with all renderings, there are inaccuracies, but the image does indicate the variety of participants in the Battle of Bennington.

THE AFTERMATH OF THE
BATTLE OF BENNINGTON

O n August 20, 1777, Burgoyne wrote to Lord Germain in England and gave a wonderful tribute to Vermont:

> *The New Hampshire Grants* [Vermont], *in particular, an area unpeopled and almost unknown in the last war, now abounds in the most active and most rebellious race on the continent, and hangs like a gathering storm on my left.*

After Bennington, colonists knew they could beat the trained British forces. Troops going to the Saratoga area swelled from three thousand in early August to over ten thousand in mid-September to nearly twenty thousand in early October. Burgoyne, already short of supplies, lost 15 percent of his troops, four cannons and other badly needed supplies at the Battle of Bennington and was forced to surrender at Saratoga two months later on October 17, 1777. His Native American friends lost confidence, his key German allies had been mauled and he never got the horses and supplies he needed.

As the noted by the British historian Trevelyan, almost two hundred years after the Battle of Bennington,

> *Bennington...proved to be the turning point of the Saratoga Campaign which was the turning point of the Revolutionary War.*

France and other nations entered the Revolutionary War on the side of the Americans. George Washington said that he was no longer worried about Burgoyne's army after the "brilliant stroke" put on by Stark and the various militia.

Thomas Jefferson, who had visited the Catamount Tavern—where Stark had met with the Council of Safety—in 1791, wrote:

> *This success was the first link in the chain of events which opened a new scene in America. It raised her from the depths of despair to the summit of hope, and added unfaded laurels to the veteran who commanded* [Stark].

British forces never again seriously threatened New England, except for a few raids.

Stark went on to serve at Saratoga and returned to New Hampshire via Route 9 in Vermont, now called Molly Stark Highway after his wife. Stark retired after Saratoga and lived to be ninety-four. Stark, along with Ethan Allen, have their statues in Statuary Hall in Washington.

Late in life, Stark turned down a request to attend a reunion at Bennington of the soldiers at the Battle of Bennington. In turning down this request due to health, he offered a toast: "Live free or die. Death is not the worst of evils." In 1945, New Hampshire made "Live Free or Die" the state motto, and it has been on New Hampshire license plates ever since.

Warner eventually returned to Connecticut for persistent health issues and died at age forty-one. Route 30, out of Manchester toward Fort Ticonderoga, is named the Seth Warner Memorial Highway and a monument marks the spot.

General St. Clair went on to face a court-martial for abandoning Fort Ticonderoga without firing a shot. He was acquitted and later became president of the Continental Congress.

General Lincoln came back to Bennington after the Battle of Bennington and devised a plan to harass the rear guard on Burgoyne during August, September and October 1777. He marched north again through Bennington County and based his army with Herrick in Pawlet, the first town out of Bennington County.

Over a hundred years later on a regional basis, and with federal help, the 306-foot Bennington Battle Monument was built on the site of the Continental storehouse that the British were trying to capture. The view from the top includes the Vermont Valley to Manchester in the north over twenty miles away.

The Aftermath of the Battle of Bennington

"LIVE FREE OF DIE," NEW HAMPSHIRE
This motto has a tie to Bennington. It was John Stark's toast for a reunion of Battle of Bennington veterans. He said "Live free or die. Death is not the worst of evils." Since 1945, New Hampshire has adopted the first part of the toast as its state motto. *Photo by author. Courtesy of Hemmings.*

"THE BENNINGTON FLAG"
Note the unique seven-pointed stars and the white stripes on the outside. The original hangs in a protective case in the Bennington Museum. It has become associated with the victory at the Battle of Bennington and many homes and businesses still fly this flag.

BATTLE OF BENNINGTON COMMEMORATIVE U.S. POSTAGE STAMPS
This 1927 stamp was issued 150 years after the Battle of Bennington and is a tribute to the Green Mountain Boys' role at the Battle of Bennington. Notice the attire of the Green Mountain Boy.

Bennington Shaft...
Bennington National Cemetary
Point Loma, Calif. #120

USS BENNINGTON MONUMENT, POINT LOMA, SAN DIEGO, CALIFORNIA
The first USS *Bennington* was a gunboat commissioned in 1891. It had a fire and sixty-two sailors died. Some of the dead were placed here in Port Loma with an obelisk (dedicated in 1908) to commemorate the event. The cemetery was called the Bennington National Cemetery. It is now part of the Fort Rosecrans National Cemetery. *U.S. government photo.*

The Aftermath of the Battle of Bennington

USS *Bennington*

The second naval vessel to be named for the Battle of Bennington was this historic aircraft carrier. It was involved in many historic events, including fighting kamikazes in the Pacific during World War II. A bell from the ship is on display in Bennington outside the town hall. It was commissioned on August 6, 1944, and decommissioned on January 15, 1970. *U.S. government photo.*

The green flag with stars (shown in the back cover image) is still used today by the Vermont National Guard and New Hampshire. The stars and stripes flag, with the "76" shown by the stars, was thought to have been made to commemorate the Battle of Bennington (an original is in the Bennington Museum) and is still flown in Bennington County at homes and businesses. It is advertised as the "Bennington flag." It was the only stars and stripes flag with the white stripes on the outside and seven pointed stars.

The U.S. government named two warships the USS *Bennington*. The first was a gunboat, and it was the sister ship of gunboats *Lexington* and *Concord*. A smaller monument, similar in design to the 306-foot-tall monument in Bennington, was erected in Port Loma (near San Diego) in the Bennington National Cemetery to honor the dead of the first USS *Bennington* (the cemetery is now part of the Fort Rosecrans National Cemetery). The second USS *Bennington* was an aircraft carrier commissioned on August 6,

1944, that fought off kamikaze attacks in 1945 during World War II. The bell from the USS *Bennington* is displayed in Bennington.

The United States produced a postage stamp in 1927 commemorating the role of the Green Mountain Boys at the Battle of Bennington.

Burgoyne faced an inquiry in London on the "expedition" from Canada. His description and the testimony of the battle events are available for everyone to read.

Starksboro, Vermont, was named after John Stark. In appreciation for the help of Colonel Simonds of Massachusetts in the Battle of Bennington, he was given a town in Vermont. He named it Lincoln after Benjamin Lincoln. Also, Seth Warner's widow was given land in northern Vermont, now called Warner's Grant (some have said it should be Warners Grant).

Both Stark and Burgoyne used storm analogies after the Battle of Bennington. Stark said the battle was a "continual clap of thunder." Burgoyne said that Vermont "[hung] like a gathering storm on my left" as he moved south. The battle was not the "shot heard round the world," but it may have been the shot heard on two continents.

The independent Republic of Vermont, in 1791, became the fourteenth state, the first state admitted after the original thirteen.

TOURS IN BENNINGTON COUNTY

THE SITES OF THESE EVENTS

The following self-guided tours are designed so that the traveler may start anywhere and do one tour at a time, leaving the others for later, or combine the tours together. Due to the nature of history, many of the events occurred up and down Route Historic 7A, so a loop-type tour is not practical.

It is also suggested that the traveler contact the various Bennington County organizations to see if any related events are occurring when you are there. Suggestions include: Bennington Chamber of Commerce (www.Bennington.com), Manchester Chamber of Commerce (www. manchestervermont.net) and Hildene (www.Hildene.org). There are frequent reenactments, such as Ethan Allen Days and Battle of Bennington ceremonies.

OLD BENNINGTON, VT

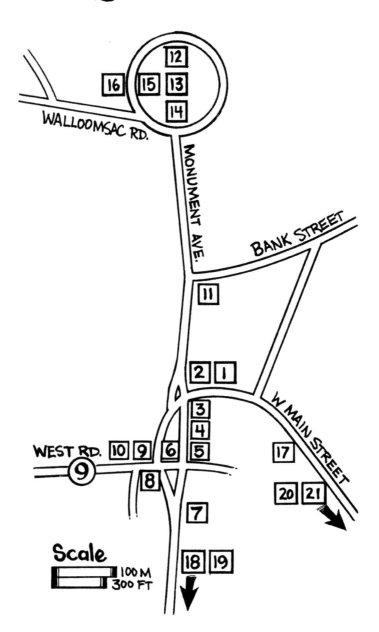

OLD BENNINGTON MAP
This map shows the sites in Old Bennington that were significant in both Ethan Allen's march north to capture Fort Ticonderoga in 1775 and the march south of troops to the Battle of Bennington in 1777.

OLD BENNINGTON

Sites 1 through 17 on the Old Bennington map can be walked, but sites 18 through 21 probably require a car. The walk along Monument Avenue from the Catamount Tavern monument (number 2) to the Bennington Battle Monument is very pretty and has many homes from the 1700s and 1800s. The area from the Bennington Battle Monument down Monument Avenue and on the side streets is in the Old Bennington District on the National Register of Historic Places. Many of the homes have historic markers on them.

If you follow the history and understand that Ethan Allen, in 1775, started at the Catamount Tavern, and John Stark, Seth Warner and others planned the Battle of Bennington at the Catamount Tavern, this is a natural place to start the tour. Walking this area will give more meaning to the history and events behind the Bennington Battle Monument built over a hundred years after the Battle of Bennington. Although there is considerable history in this area, this tour highlights the sights that were pertinent to the events of 1775 and 1777.

In season, there is a public restroom and parking at the gift center area next to the 306-foot-tall Bennington Battle Monument.

1. CATAMOUNT TAVERN SITE

Green Mountain Tavern (see image on page 26) or Fay's Tavern (it was operated by Stephen Fay) was built around 1767–69, but a fire destroyed it in 1871. It was about forty-five feet east of the Catamount Tavern monument (number 2). It was a two-story wood structure that had a stuffed catamount in front facing west toward New York. It had an unpainted look on the outside, and inside it had a "council room." This was where Ethan Allen and the Green Mountain Boys would drink their "stonewalls"(rum and hard cider). Ethan Allen formed the Green Mountain Boys here and the tavern became their headquarters from 1770–75. It was also here, in May 1775, that Heman Allen informed Ethan Allen that a group was coming from Connecticut and Massachusetts to ask him to lead a march to Ticonderoga. Allen left the tavern to march north to capture Fort Ticonderoga.

In 1777, John Stark made his headquarters here prior to the Battle of Bennington, and on the morning of August 16, tradition has it that Stark got up in the morning, got on his horse and road off to victory at the Battle of Bennington. The Council of Safety (Vermont's only form of government at the time) also met here to manage the state and the British invasion during July and August 1777. It was here that the British officer prisoners from the Battle of Bennington were temporarily kept. According to some recollections, about two hundred feet to the south of the tavern is where a temporary "hospital" was set up to treat the wounded from the Battle of Bennington. The current home on the site is a private residence.

2. CATAMOUNT TAVERN MONUMENT

The polished brown granite monument on Monument Avenue Granite Base has a solid bronze catamount—a species of American panther—on the top, facing west toward New York. The six- by two-foot base tapers to seven feet in height. G. Moretti sculpted it. This monument stands directly opposite the front door of the Catamount Tavern. About four rods (sixty-six feet) south of the monument is where the original signpost with the stuffed catamount on top stood.

CATAMOUNT TAVERN MONUMENT, BENNINGTON
This marker on Monument Avenue is situated almost directly in front of where the Catamount Tavern main door was located. It is also near the pole that had the stuffed catamount on it. Notice that the catamount is snarling and facing west.

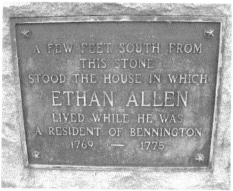

ETHAN ALLEN HOME MARKER, BENNINGTON
Ethan Allen lived in Bennington for the six years prior to his march from Bennington to capture Fort Ticonderoga. The marker is on the corner of Route 9 and Monument Avenue. The marker is about fifty feet from where Allen lived and across the street from where the Catamount Tavern was located.

3. ETHAN ALLEN'S HOMESITE

On the southeast corner of where Monument Avenue crosses Route 9, there is a plaque indicating where Ethan Allen's home (see image on page 23) was located during his residency of Bennington from 1769 to 1775. The home was a two-and-half-story gambrel-style structure. The home was almost exactly where the J.G. McCollugh Mausoleum stands today. The house was eventually, at least partially, rebuilt and was used as a tin shop.

4. OLD BURYING GROUND

The Old Burying Ground, established in 1762, is the oldest in Vermont and is Vermont's "sacred acre." Robert Frost, who lived in nearby Shaftsbury, is buried here. Dr. Jonas Fay (son of the owner of the Catamount Tavern) is buried along the front fence. Dr. Fay was "author of the Vermont State Constitution" and was with Ethan Allen during the capture of Fort Ticonderoga. The headstone of Stephen Fay (1714–81), who was the owner of the Catamount Tavern, is the first headstone on the left as you enter. Isaac Techinor, who helped build up the supplies that the British were coming after in the Battle of Bennington, is buried here on the main path a few feet from the entrance. His gravestone is about twelve feet tall and resembles the 306-foot Bennington Battle Monument obelisk, which today marks the spot of the stores he was responsible for building up.

About halfway down the path, you will see a large, solid monument in an open area. This is the mass grave of the British (mainly Hessians and Brunswickers) and Americans who died in the Battle of Bennington. On the side of the monument, you will see the name of David Redding, who fought in the Battle of Bennington on the side of the British. He was hanged for allegedly

MASS GRAVE, OLD BURYING GROUND, BENNINGTON
This is the gravestone for the mass grave containing British (Germans) and Americans who died in the Battle of Bennington. It also contains the remains of David Redding (sometimes spelled Redden), who was hanged in 1778 for "enemical conduct" against Vermont during the war.

stealing supplies to give to the British. His name is also sometimes written "Redden." He was hanged across the street from the Catamount Tavern. Also, Aaron Hubbell, who was a twenty-year-old guard of the prisoners from the Battle of Bennington and whose house still stands a mile west on Route 9, is buried here with his wife. There is an excellent locator map at the entrance to the cemetery. Please show respect as you go through the cemetery.

5. OLD FIRST CHURCH
"Vermont's Colonial Shrine" was built after the Revolution and was dedicated in 1806. However, the congregation dates back to 1762 and was established by Parson Dewey, who was the preacher in 1775–77 at the first meetinghouse (see number 6). It was built over part of the old cemetery, and some of the deceased Revolutionary War participants had their remains moved. The church was built by Lavius Fillmore and is a good example of Federal-type architecture. In conjunction with the adjacent Old Burying Ground, this is one of the most photographed settings in Vermont. It is believed to be the oldest church in Vermont still standing.

6. FIRST MEETINGHOUSE SITE
A twelve- by six-foot marker lays flat at the site in the middle of the green. The first meetinghouse was built of wood on the site of the marker in 1763–65 (see rendering on page 25). It was torn down around 1806 because

the new Old First Church was built across the street. The oldest Protestant congregation in Vermont was started here, with Jedediah Dewey as pastor. Ethan Allen attended services here, although he was not always on the same page as the pastor. A prayer service was held here giving thanks to the Lord for bringing everyone back safely after the capture of Fort Ticonderoga and Ethan Allen said, "Don't forget to mention I was there." Most of the seven hundred prisoners from the Battle of Bennington were housed here before many were transferred to Massachusetts.

Not only had Ethan Allen been in this spot, but two future presidents, James Madison and Thomas Jefferson, were also here in 1791. It was also used for town meetings.

7. Parson Jedediah Dewey Home

Built around 1763, this is one of the oldest frame houses in Vermont and the oldest in the Monument Avenue historic district. Mr. Dewey, who was the first pastor of the Separatist Congregational congregation, built it. Dewey

was also a carpenter. The large central chimney and unusually wide clapboards are indicative of its early construction date. Dewey's eldest son, Elijah, built or had built the Walloomsac Inn almost diagonally across the street. The north wing of the house is newer. It is now a private residence.

PARSON JEDEDIAH DEWEY HOME, BENNINGTON
This home was built in 1763 by Parson Dewey, who was the first preacher at the first meetinghouse that was almost diagonally across the street. His son, Elijah Dewey, ran the Walloomsac Inn across the green. The Parson Dewey House is now a private residence.

8. Nathaniel Brush House

Although there have been some modifications, the house was built in 1775 (see the image for Walloomsac Inn). Nathaniel Brush, a Green Mountain Boy, was at the Battle of Bennington and, with Samuel Herrick, he left Stark's camp on Harrington Road in Bennington and sneaked around behind the British lines. The grave of Colonel Bush, who commanded the Bennington militia, is unmarked and unknown.

9. WALLOOMSAC INN

Most people seem to agree that the inn was built at least as early as 1771. It was built for (and maybe partly by) Captain Elijah Dewey (son of the pastor whose house was almost across the street). It looks today almost the way it did then, with unpainted wood siding. It had become the oldest continuously operating inn in Vermont until it became a private residence in the late twentieth century. The Berry family has owned the house for many years.

Food for the soldiers, including John Stark, at the Battle of Bennington was prepared here. Elijah Dewey served at the Battle of Bennington as a captain. A story goes that a man came up to knock on the door asking for some food during the battle. Elijah Dewey's wife scolded him for not being out with the men fighting. He then said he had just returned from Albany after driving cattle there to help the war effort. She apologized and fed him. He was Isaac Techinor, recently appointed assistant in charge of building up supplies at the storehouse. He later built a house next door and would become a multiterm governor of Vermont.

After the battle, food for some of the seven hundred prisoners was cooked here. Later, on their 1791 trip, future Presidents Thomas Jefferson and James Madison visited the inn. Even later, in 1877, Rutherford B. Hayes had a reception at the inn during ceremonies for the building of the Bennington Battle Monument. Walt Disney also stayed here and President Benjamin Harrison also visited the inn. The sign "Walloomsac Inn" is now at the Bennington Museum.

WALLOOMSAC INN AND NATHANIEL BRUSH HOUSE, BENNINGTON
Meals were cooked here for John Stark and his men before the Battle of Bennington. After the battle, food was cooked for the seven hundred British (German) prisoners who were housed across the street. It has the same basic unpainted look as it did two centuries ago. Most accounts date the inn to 1771 or earlier. The Nathaniel Brush House in the background was built in 1775. It was home to Colonel Brush, who fought with honor in the Battle of Bennington, as did Captain Dewey. Both houses are private residences now.

ISAAC TICHENOR HOUSE, BENNINGTON
Located next to the Walloomsac Inn, this was the home built circa 1790 by Isaac Tichenor. He came to Vermont in June 1777 to build up the stores that became the target of the attack by British (German) troops. After taking cattle to Albany, he returned just after the battle. It is now a private home.

10. ISAAC TICHENOR HOUSE

Although built after 1777 (about 1790), the house is important because it was built by Isaac Tichenor, who was responsible for building up supplies at the continental storehouse. It was these supplies that were the temptation to the British prior to the Battle of Bennington. Near the northeast corner of the house, Tory David Redding was hanged and his remains are in the mass grave in the Old Burying Grounds (number 4). He was alleged to have been stealing some of the supplies. Apparently, this was the first public "hanging" in Vermont. The house is now a private residence.

11. FIRST LOG HOUSE MARKER

On the southwest corner of Monument Avenue and Bank Street is a marker describing the log cabin built by Samuel Robinson, the leader of the first settlers in Bennington. In a drawing for *Vermont Life* (see image on page 20) Robinson's wife is shown chasing off wolves in 1767, only eight years before Ethan Allen marched north to Ticonderoga in 1775. The marker was unveiled on August 16, 1923, by Deacon Samuel L. Robinson, a descendant of Samuel Robinson. The mission to England referenced on the marker was to get the Crown to protect the current settlers' land rights against New York claims.

12. JOHN STARK STATUE

General John Stark from New Hampshire had overall command of the forces at the victory at the Battle of Bennington. He responded to Vermont's pleas for help from the invading British. The statue shows one version of the famous quote regarding Molly Stark sleeping a widow if they didn't win. The actual spot of the famous quote is shown in the Bennington Battle Theater tour. Note that Stark is pointing west, which is the direction of the Battle of Bennington. If you see New Hampshire license plates in the area, remember the motto, "Live Free or Die," was from John Stark as part of his toast for the reunion of Battle of Bennington soldiers in the early 1800s.

BENNINGTON BATTLE MONUMENT, BENNINGTON

Over 306 feet tall, the battle monument was dedicated in 1891. It has an elevator for visitors. In the foreground is the memorial statue for Seth Warner, leader of the Green Mountain Boys and one of the heroes of the Battle of Bennington. Olin Scott, in 1911, erected the Seth Warner statue. The monument is administered by the State of Vermont.

13. BENNINGTON BATTLE MONUMENT

The monument was built in 1887–91 to commemorate the overwhelming victory of Patriot forces at the Battle of Bennington. The monument is just over 306 feet. Currently inside is a camp kettle captured from General Burgoyne after his surrender at Saratoga. There is also a diorama of the second engagement of the Battle of Bennington that involved Seth Warner. The monument is now state operated, and there is an elevator to the top. Many people, including President Benjamin Harrison, dedicated it on August 19, 1891. The main architect was by John Phillip Rinn of Boston. There is an excellent book by Tyler Resch titled *Bennington's Battle Monument: Massive and Lofty*, which shows all the designs considered and the monument's history.

If you walk to the west of the monument toward the gift shop and look north, you will get a sense of another major event. When Ethan Allen and the expedition left the Catamount Tavern (number 1), they essentially came up what is now Monument Avenue, crossed where you are standing and then headed north down the hill across the Walloomsac River (there used to be a covered bridge there). They then went up Harwood Hill Road (now Historic 7A) and then north up the Vermont Valley to capture Fort Ticonderoga seventy miles away.

14. Seth Warner Statue

The nine-foot obelisk shaft in front of the Bennington Battle Monument supports a larger-than-life image of Warner, who resided in Bennington from 1765 for about another twenty years (see Bennington Battle Monument image). Warner was the Bennington farmer of modest wealth and social position who was the undisputed field commander of Vermont's regiment of rangers in the Continental army. His home and farm were in Bennington and are indicated in the Bennington Battle Theater tour. Prior to the Revolution, Warner was one of the brash leaders of the Green Mountain Boys. He was one of the true heroes of the Battle of Bennington when his Green Mountain Boys arrived from Manchester at the last minute and saved the second engagement at the Battle of Bennington. He was also with Ethan Allen at the capture of Fort Ticonderoga and led the forces almost immediately afterward in capturing the British fort at Crown Point.

15. New Hampshire/Massachusetts Markers

These markers explain the role of the various troops from these states in the Battle of Bennington and recognize the contributions of the leaders. Colonel Simonds (Massachusetts) and Colonel Nichols (New Hampshire) are recognized.

16. Continental Storehouse Site

A granite marker on Monument Circle marks the spot where this two-story wood building once stood. It contained the supplies for the American army that the British were coming to retrieve when they were repulsed at the Battle

of Bennington. It was demolished to make room for the Bennington Battle Monument park area. The stores were built up by Isaac Techinor and included livestock, such as cattle and horses. It is presumed that these were guarded on the nearby farmland.

Looking north and east down the hill is the current Mount Anthony golf course that gives a feel for what the grazing areas looked like. The map at the Old Burying Ground (number 4) shows how

Continental Stores Marker, Bennington
Located near the Battle of Bennington Monument, this marker indicates where the storehouse was that the British were trying to capture for supplies. The storehouse is no longer there.

open the area was even a hundred years after the Battle of Bennington. It also is assumed that there were other buildings used for some of the Northern Army's supplies. The Battle of Bennington bicentennial literature indicated that the stores were probably spread out in adjacent nearby barns so that, in the event of attack or fire, all would not be lost.

17. BENNINGTON MUSEUM

The museum has parking, but it is an easy walk from the Old Burying Ground as the museum abuts the back of the Old Burying Ground. The museum contains a vast collection of Battle of Bennington mementos, including one of the cannons captured at the battle. The full mural by Leroy Williams (about twelve feet by six feet) shown on the cover is on display there with a complete explanation and identification of the people, uniforms and so forth. An original "76" Bennington flag (see picture on page 97) is also there, as is the green flag with the white stars reported to be flown at the Battle of Bennington (see image on back cover). Other artifacts also include parts of the Catamount Tavern and the first meetinghouse. There is also a well-respected research library with many original documents and a good diagram of the battle itself. The museum contains a section dedicated to Grandma Moses, who lived in the area.

18. MILE MARKER

From the Old First Church (number 5), go south on Monument Avenue about one mile. Just past the entrance to Southern Vermont College on the lawn is a mile marker. These mile markers were to indicate the distance to Bennington for travelers from the south. This marker was probably moved and it may have been originally placed after 1777, but it does seem to indicate the growing importance of the route up from Route 7 to Old Bennington. North of Bennington, the markers show the distance from Bennington. At least five of these mile markers are still in existence—in Dorset, Manchester, Arlington, Shaftsbury and Bennington. Some sources have said that some markers were placed as early as 1775.

19. JEWETT HOUSE

The Jewett House is about two miles south of the mile marker in number 18. At the end of Monument Avenue and Route 7, it is another quarter

JEWETT HOUSE, BENNINGTON
Built in 1770 as a house-tavern, it is situated at a fork in the north-south road. Just past the tavern, early travelers could go north to Bennington Center (Old Bennington) via today's Monument Avenue or go straight into the emerging east section of town. The front is the original part of the house. It is now a private residence.

mile on the right. Built around 1770 originally as a tavern, this is one of the earliest structures remaining along the Route 7 corridor and is a point where the northbound road splits, with one route going to Old Bennington and the other route going to current Bennington. The front section served as a tavern. The Jewett family owned the house for most of the nineteenth century. The expedition going north to Bennington in 1775 may have passed this tavern. The house is a private residence now.

20. USS BENNINGTON BELL (TOWN OFFICES)
The bell from the USS *Bennington* aircraft carrier is on display outside the town hall. Over the years, thousands of men and women served on this ship, which fought kamikaze attacks during World War II and received many awards. From the Bennington Museum (number 17), take Route 9 east into the center of town and turn right at the traffic light (south on Route 7). The bell is about a hundred yards south on the right.

21. LIEUTENANT COLONEL SAMUEL SAFFORD HOUSE
The house is located at 722 Main (East), right in downtown Bennington. This home (now the Samuel Safford Inn) traces its roots back to at least 1774, indicating that there were some homes in this part of town in 1775. Note in the front section the single chimney in the center that was common in Revolutionary War era. Samuel Safford brought the Green Mountain Boys reinforcements south from Manchester in the rain on August 15, 1777, and Seth Warner led them on August 16 in the second engagement of the Battle of Bennington.

BENNINGTON BATTLE THEATER

This is a tour of the main sites in Bennington that were involved in the Battle of Bennington in 1777. The tour requires a car and starts in Old Bennington. It would be helpful to first take the tour of Old Bennington. This tour could be done in a loop, returning to Old Bennington.

1. STARK'S HEADQUARTERS, CATAMOUNT TAVERN

The entire area around the green was involved in the Battle of Bennington before, during and after the battle. The Council of Safety, which was the governing body of Vermont, was in session, holding meetings at the Catamount Tavern in its "council room" (see image on page 26). Later, British (German) officers who were prisoners were kept at the Catamount. Across the street, food was prepared for Stark's troops at the Walloomsac Inn (still in existence) and the Walloomsac owner, Elijah Dewey, fought in the battle. To the left of the Walloomsac Inn was the Nathaniel Brush House (still in existence). Brush also fought in the Battle of Bennington. The Old Burying Ground has the mass grave of people who fought in the battle and died. The grave of Aaron Hubbell, who brought the prisoners back to Bennington, is also visible. In the center of the green is the marker indicating the first meetinghouse, where many of the seven hundred prisoners where housed and the wounded were treated.

With the British moving south, the activity in the weeks before the Battle of Bennington in this little village can only be imagined. Stark was coming and going. Refugees from the north were coming through on the

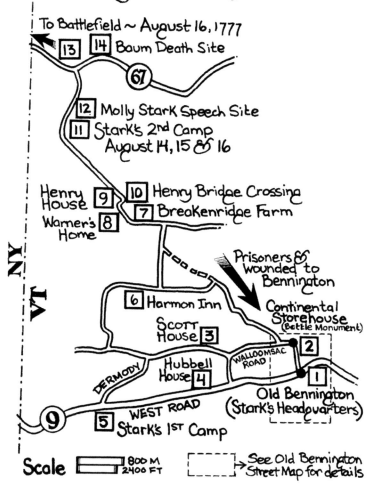

BENNINGTON BATTLE THEATER AUGUST 1777

Bennington County, Vermont

To Battlefield ~ August 16, 1777

[13] [14] Baum Death Site

(67)

[12] Molly Stark Speech Site
[11] Stark's 2nd Camp
August 14, 15 & 16

Henry [9] [10] Henry Bridge Crossing
House [8] [7] Breakenridge Farm
Warner's
Home

NY
VT

Prisoners & wounded to Bennington

[6] Harmon Inn

Scott House [3]

Continental Storehouse (Battle Monument)

DERMODY
Hubbell House [4]
WALLOOMSAC ROAD

[2]

[1]

(9) WEST ROAD
[5] Stark's 1st Camp

Old Bennington (Stark's Headquarters)

Scale [800 M / 2400 FT]

See Old Bennington Street Map for details

BENNINGTON BATTLE THEATER
The map identifies the location of sites in Bennington County that were part of the Bennington battle theater.

way to safety in Massachusetts. The Council of Safety met constantly, sending messengers on horseback to get more troops and ammunition. Finally, on August 16, 1777, the day of the battle, General Stark emerged from the Catamount, mounted his horse and rode west to the battle.

2. CONTINENTAL STOREHOUSE

The Continental Storehouse, where the 306-foot Bennington Battle Monument is today, was a temptation to the British. There is a marker on the exact spot (see picture page 111).

PHINEAS SCOTT HOUSE, BENNINGTON
Built at least as early as 1772, tradition says that bread for the soldiers from the Battle of Bennington was cooked here in the large fireplace. It is now a private residence.

3. PHINEAS SCOTT HOUSE

Built at least as early as 1772 for his bride, Thankful Kinsley, this is a classic New England saltbox. It is said that after the Battle of Bennington, bread was baked for the Green Mountain Boys in its huge central fireplace. From the Bennington Battle Monument, it is about one mile west on the right. It is now a private residence.

4. AARON HUBBELL HOUSE

Take Walloomsac Road back east to Gypsy Lane, then south to Route 9 (West Road) and west about a mile—on the right is the Hubbell Homestead, built in 1768. Aaron Hubbell was only twenty when he was asked to escort and guard some of the seven hundred prisoners back to Bennington. He is shown in the cover image on the far right prodding prisoners. There is a bullet hole in a door (now inside) that a descendent, Katherine Hubbell, says is from the gun of a "Hessian scout" prior to the Battle of Bennington. There may be some validity to this statement since both sides used spies extensively and this house was on a road leading to the supply depot in Bennington. Most likely, it

AARON HUBBELL HOUSE, BENNINGTON
Built at least as early as 1768, this was the home of Aaron Hubbell, who was one of the guards taking some of the seven hundred prisoners back to the first meetinghouse in Bennington, about one mile east down the road. He is portrayed in the cover image on the far right, prodding Tory prisoners. It is now a private home, but it is available for special occasions such as weddings.

was not a "Hessian," but the Germans did employ local Tory scouts to avoid detection. Further research is needed. The homestead offers a great view of the agricultural lands and the mountains that are still here today. Katherine Hubbell lived across the street from the Hubbell homestead. The homestead is under private ownership.

5. DIMMICK TAVERN MARKER
The Dimmick Tavern (Stand) was built at least as early as 1772 by Hendrick Schnieder. During the five-day encampment of General Stark's troops from August 9 to August 13, it was owned and managed by Colonel Herrick, an officer under Colonel Stark. Herrick was head of the Green Mountain Rangers. Stark went back (about two miles east on Route 9) to Bennington for meetings with the Council of Safety. For at least seventy-five years, it was known as Dimmick's Tavern or Stand ("stand" was an old expression for a stage stop). The State of New Hampshire erected a marker in 1927. The tavern itself was destroyed by fire on November 10, 1869. Some later spellings have "Dimick" with one *m*.

DIMMICK HOUSE MARKER, BENNINGTON
This marker indicates where General Stark's troops had a five-day camp August 9–13 before moving to a new camp. The marker is visible from Route 9 in Bennington. Colonel Herrick, a hero at the Battle of Bennington, lived in the house that became known as Dimmick's Stand (Tavern).

6. DANIEL HARMON INN SITE

From Dimmick Tavern, take Demoody to Walloomsac and turn left on Whipstock and then Vail Road. On the corner of Vail and Airport, there is small marker. General Stark and staff supposedly ate at the inn on August 14, 1777, which is the day he was moving north to set up his new camp (see image page 89). The building was torn down in 1922. It was also the birthplace of Canadian explorer Daniel Williams Harmon. This area used to be a more trafficked route for travelers from the north heading south.

7. JAMES BRECKENRIDGE FARM

Continue on Vail Road, make left on Austin Hill and then make a left on Murphy for a short distance. The stone monument indicates where, on July 19, 1771, over three hundred New Yorkers led by the Albany sheriff Ten Eyck tried to evict James Breckenridge from his farm, saying his New Hampshire grant was not valid. It was Bennington residents, including Seth Warner, who repulsed the Yorkers. Breckenridge was an anti-Yorker, but as times would have it, he became a Loyalist in the Revolution. He spent six months in a Litchfield gaol (prison) but was allowed to return to his home after the war. He is buried in the Old Burying Ground in Old Bennington.

8. SETH WARNER HOUSE

Near the descriptive marker is where Colonel Seth Warner lived in Bennington (see picture on page 89). Warner was the leader of the Green Mountain Boys and a hero of the Battle of Bennington. His knowledge of the battle theater helped Stark. Warner's house was similar to the existing Henry House less than a half mile up the road. Warner died in 1784.

THE HENRY HOUSE, BENNINGTON
The house was built in 1769 as a residence. The architecture is similar to that of the Seth Warner home just down the road. Lieutenant William Henry, who fought in the Battle of Bennington, resided here. It is now an inn.

9. HENRY HOUSE

The house was originally built in 1769. It had a strategic location because considerable southbound traffic crossed at this section of the Walloomsac River that is fairly shallow. It is similar in design to the Seth Warner House that used to be just to the north (see number 8). It is said that Aaron Hubbell lived in the house before living in his other Bennington home (see number 4). On August 14, 1777, on the way to the Battle of Bennington, Aaron Hubbell's unit was asked to fell trees near here to block the advance of the British. Aaron Hubbell, at the age of twenty, felled the first tree. Lieutenant William Henry also lived in the house; he fought in the Battle of Bennington. Land for the home was purchased from James Breckenridge. It is currently run as a bed-and-breakfast.

10. HENRY BRIDGE CROSSING

This was a good crossing for troops. It is on the path from General Stark's first camp in the south at Dimmick's Tavern to his second camp to the north on Harrington Road. Troops coming down from Manchester that went into Bennington and then out to the Battle of Bennington would cross the meandering Walloomsac River here.

HENRY BRIDGE CROSSING, BENNINGTON
The covered bridge was not there in 1777, but this is the spot where troops from
Manchester crossed the Walloomsac River on their way to the Battle of Bennington.
There is a historic marker adjacent to the crossing.

11. STARK'S ENCAMPMENT, AUGUST 14–16

The marker on Harrington Road (Bennington) indicates the site where Stark
camped after moving his camp from Dimmick's Tavern (see picture on page
91). Facing west toward the hills of New York, from this spot Vermont's
Herrick and Brush took over two hundred Vermonters and went to the left
on August 16 to get behind the British. At the same time, Colonel Nichols
from New Hampshire went right and traveled six miles around the back of
the British. Nichols actually passed through Shaftsbury (Vermont) on the
way to his position behind the British. Patrols moving out could see Baum's
encampment area only a couple of miles from here. The hill itself probably
blocked a direct view of Baum's positions. Parson Allen (the fighting parson
from Massachusetts) arrived here to demand a fight. With Stark being from
New Hampshire, it is somewhat ironic that those going north to the battle
would have passed through the land Benning Wentworth reserved for himself
when he created Bennington as the first town in today's Vermont.

12. STARK SPEECH SPOT

Sources indicate that it was "some twenty rods" or about 325 feet from the
place of the encampment here that Stark made his "Molly Stark" speech,
probably on the road where his troops were forming. There is disagreement
among authorities as to whether he was on horseback or stood on the
topmost rail of a fence. There are many versions of the speech; former

Governor Hiland Hall, who was also a historian, favors: "There are the red coats, and they are ours or this night Molly Stark sleeps a widow."

13. BENNINGTON BATTLEFIELD, WALLOOMSAC, NEW YORK

BENNINGTON BATTLEFIELD ENTRANCE, WALLOOMSAC, NEW YORK
The entrance to the New York State Bennington Battlefield Historic Site is on Route 67, about two miles west of Bennington in New York. Some of the battle engagements are outside the historic site, such as Seth Warner's engagement with British reinforcements. The visitor center is also outside the park on Caretakers Road, where there were other engagements near the Walloomsac River.

Take Harrington Road north to Route 67 West. This route leaves current-day Vermont, and after about two miles, you will see the sign for the Bennington Battlefield on the right. The battlefield operation is seasonal, so check the website for hours of operation. In addition, about a hundred yards east from the park entrance is Caretakers Road. At the end of Caretakers, by the Walloomsac River, some of the battle engagements took place. Also, about a mile west of the park entrance, there is a three-foot marker by the Bennington Paperboard Plant indicating how far Seth Warner pursued the retreating British reinforcements. There are good displays in the park, as well as at the visitor center, which has some very good aerial photos of the entire battle theater.

14. SITE OF HOUSE WHERE BAUM DIED, SHAFTSBURY, VERMONT.

Lieutenant Colonel Friedrich Baum (the commander of the British [German] expedition to Bennington) along with Colonel Pfister (Head of the Tories) were taken to this wooden house, which is about a mile east of the battlefield park. There is a marker at the site on the north side of route 67. Pfister was carried on the back of one of Stark's veterans, and he died within a few hours of his commander, Baum. Baum was buried on the bank of the Walloomsac River, but the exact spot is not known (see image on page 93).

BENNINGTON TO MANCHESTER (INCLUDES SHAFTSBURY, ARLINGTON, SUNDERLAND)

This tour leaves from Bennington via Route Historic 7A and goes north through the towns of Shaftsbury, Arlington and Sunderland before arriving in Manchester. Route Historic 7A, in sections, had different locations, but the general corridor up or down the Vermont Valley is the same as it has been for over two hundred years. This is the basic route taken by Ethan Allen as he marched north to capture Fort Ticonderoga in 1775 and by John Stark and the Green Mountain Boys as they traveled south to the Battle of Bennington. By following the distances between sites and the site descriptions, the tour is structured so a traveler could do the reverse and go from Manchester to Bennington.

HARWOOD HILL

From Northshire Drive in Bennington, go up Harwood Hill Road (this is also Historic 7A) about half a mile. About halfway up the hill before Hunter's Restaurant, there is a view of the Bennington Battle Monument. According to owners, in 1763 Zacheria Harwood bought seventy-four acres and established an orchard here. Zacheria was a Revolutionary War soldier. Memoirs of soldiers on the way to the Battle of Bennington indicated that troops rested at the farm and refreshed themselves with cider. There is still an orchard in the area. The troops apparently then went the next mile or so to get supplies at the storehouse (located where the Bennington Battle Monument is today) and headed west toward the battle.

SHAFTSBURY

ROBERT FROST HOUSE, SHAFTSBURY
Built in 1769, this house would have been visible to the expedition going to Fort Ticonderoga in 1775 and also to the troops going south to the Battle of Bennington in 1777. It is now a museum honoring Robert Frost, who lived in the house from 1920 to 1929. He composed "Stopping by Woods on a Snowy Evening" while residing in the house.

Robert Frost House

About one and a half miles from the Harwood Hill area is the house that was built by Amaziah Martin in 1769. The house today is the well-marked Robert Frost Museum. Frost lived there in the 1920s and wrote his famous poem "Stopping by the Woods on a Snowy Evening." Both the Fort Ticonderoga expedition going north and the Stark soldiers going south would have passed the house on Historic 7A. The year 1769 is chiseled in the ridgepole.

Parker Cole House

About a mile north of the Robert Frost Museum is Buck Hill Road at a blinking light in South Shaftsbury. A few hundred yards east on Buck Hill, on the south side, is a half-tone house built in 1770 (see earlier picture of the house on page 85). The house was used to store munitions for the Americans during the Revolution and still retains some of the solid features. In 1777, Stark's troops made mention of stopping in Shaftsbury prior to the Battle of Bennington, so they may have obtained some munitions here. It is private residence now with some attractive features added.

Waldo Tavern Site

About two and a half miles north from Buck Hill Road on Historic 7A, there is, on the left, a very distinctive and architecturally attractive brick house with a large, single, white column at the front left. (The house is privately owned.) Some of the Green Mountain Boys (probably only a few) are reported to have camped in the back field to the left near the Waldo Tavern (which no longer exists). It was at the Waldo Tavern where prayers during the Battle of Bennington were made.

Waldo Tavern Stable

Local lore, according to the National Register of Historic Places, indicates that the stable almost directly in the back of the "single, white column" house was where Seth Warner's troops rested their "remounts" prior to the Battle of Bennington.

ABIATHAR AND RACHEL WALDO HOUSE, SHAFTSBURY Built around 1765, it is one of the oldest homes in Vermont. It apparently was used to store meat during the Revolutionary War. It is now a private residence.

Abiathar and Rachel Waldo House

A few houses north of the white column house is one of "the oldest homesteads" in Vermont, having been built around 1765. Meat was possibly stored here for participants in the Battle of Bennington. Meat hooks still existed in the cellar long after the Revolution. Abiathar was a captain during the Revolutionary War and allowed his tavern to be used as a shelter for women and children. The house is now privately owned.

David Galusha Inn

Just north of the Waldo House is the Galusha Tavern, which is referenced in the journal of the expedition going north to capture Fort Ticonderoga. It was built around 1775 (see image on page 40). The inn had eighteenth-century features such as handmade nails in the attic and basement. David Galusha was the older brother of Jonas Galusha, whose homestead is just up the road north on Historic 7A. David Galusha was in the Fourth Company of the regiment of Green Mountain Boys. The Galushas had apparently just arrived in Shaftsbury in the early spring of 1775. Like the Abiathar Waldo House, this home stored supplies (in this case flour) for the Revolutionary War effort. The house is privately owned now.

Cemetery

Across the street, next to the church (Shaftsbury Historical Society), is the cemetery that traces its beginnings back to 1769. The troops headed north and south in 1775 and 1777 would have passed this cemetery. David and Jonas Galusha, as well as Abiathar Waldo, are buried here.

Carpenter House

As a side trip, at the church head about two miles west on West Mountain Road. Just before Bennett Hill Road on the right, looking up, is the restored 1765 Carpenter House. This house is featured in the book *Ordinary Heroes*, and it has been maintained and preserved by the Knapp family. It is one of the oldest houses in Shaftsbury. On West Mountain Road, the Bennington Battle Monument, about six miles away, is clearly visible. The house is a private residence.

1769 House

This home, about half a mile north of West Mountain Road, would have been visible to any of the group on Historic 7A in 1775 or 1777. It has been known as the Niles House, but has no confirmed specific Revolutionary War affiliation in the years 1775 or 1777. It is a private residence.

Jonas Galusha Homestead/Marker

Just north of the 1769, the Galusha Homestead is easily identified because of the historic sign in front. Although Jonas Galusha built the home after 1777, he and his brother were in the area from 1775 on, and both were Green Mountain Boys and fought in the Battle of Bennington. Jonas was with the group that marched around the rear of Baum's at the Battle of Bennington. It is a private residence now. Jonas went on to be a multiterm governor of Vermont.

ARLINGTON

St. James Church/Cemetery

Next to the Episcopalian church in the center of Arlington (on the corner of Historic 7A and Route 313 West) is the cemetery in which Ethan Allen's first wife, Mary Brownson, is buried.

Tory Lane

About a mile on 313 West, there is the sign for Tory Lane. This street is symbolic of Arlington being called, at times, "Tory Hollow."

TORY LANE, ARLINGTON.
This road is a reminder that, during the Revolution, Arlington had many Tories and was known as "Tory Hollow." Arlington also was home to Ethan Allen, Remember Baker and other Green Mountain Boys.

HAWLEY-CROFUT HOUSE-TAVERN, ARLINGTON.
This house also served as tavern and was built in 1773 by or for Hawley. Although Hawley became a Tory, it was a place that both Green Mountain Boys and Tories could meet. It is now a private residence.

Hawley-Crofut House

On the right, farther west on 313 West but just before River Road, is the Hawley-Crofut House. This house was originally built by or for Abel Hawley at least as early as 1773 as a tavern, but he also lived there. Dr. George Russell, a respected local historian, felt that this was the oldest surviving house in Arlington. Hawley became a Tory and his property was seized. It is possible that the house was visited by the expedition going north to capture Fort Ticonderoga. It is now a private residence.

Side Tour

Continuing west on Route 313 a few miles, there is a covered bridge and the former home/studio of Norman Rockwell (now the inn on Covered Bridge Green), where he lived for many years. The current Route 313 corridor along the Batten Kill (River) goes through the gap in the mountains that Burgoyne had originally instructed Baum's raiding party to take to Vermont. He later changed the target to Bennington.

Ethan Allen's Homesite

Back in Arlington, about a hundred yards south of the

cemetery, is East Arlington Road. After about another hundred yards on East Arlington Road, the bluish gray Mason's Hall has two plaques in the front. The one on the left indicates the spot where Ethan Allen's home was located while he lived in Arlington. The other plaque shows where Thomas Chittenden, president of the Council of Safety in 1777, lived. He was a Green Mountain Boy and the first governor of Vermont.

TORY HOUSE, ARLINGTON
This house was used to hide Tories (residents who sympathized with the Crown) during the Revolutionary War. It is very near where the Green Mountain Boy, Remember Baker, had his gristmill. The house is now privately owned.

Tory Hiding House

About a mile east on East Arlington Road, in the village of East Arlington, the red building on the right has a National Register of Historic Places plaque indicating that this was a hiding place for Tories during the Revolution.

Remember Baker Plaque

Next door, on the property of the Gristmill Antiques, is a plaque honoring Remember Baker, who was a fervent Green Mountain Boy and Ethan Allen's cousin and good friend. Baker was with Allen at the capture of Fort Ticonderoga. The plaque indicates where the gristmill that he built was located. There is also a National Register of Historic Places plaque on door of the Gristmill Antiques. Baker came to Arlington in 1764. The Gristmill Antiques is privately owned by the Keelans, who have been active in preserving history. Baker went to Canada after the capture of Fort Ticonderoga and was killed in 1775, becoming the first American to be killed in Canada during the Revolution. There is a plaque for him in Noyan, Canada.

SUNDERLAND

Ira Allen House
North on Historic 7A, about three miles from Arlington, is the Ira Allen House. Built at least as early as 1779, it served as the home of both Ethan Allen and Ira Allen. Across the road is an area where there had been a

IRA ALLEN HOUSE, SUNDERLAND
The Allen families lived in Sunderland as the marker indicates. The left part of the building with the center chimney is the older section. The house is at least as old as 1779. Ethan Allen also lived in this house. It is currently a bed-and-breakfast on Historic 7A.

IRA ALLEN CEMETERY, SUNDERLAND
Ira Allen owned land in Sunderland. The picture is taken from the Hill Farm Inn. Mount Equinox is in the background and Historic 7A is just beyond the cemetery over the little rise.

smaller building that acted as Ira Allen's office. Ethan Allen apparently wrote his book, *Reason: The Only Oracle of Man*, here and gave the first copy to his second wife, Frances Buchanan. The home is currently operated as an inn.

Ira Allen Cemetery
North a few hundred yards is Hill Farm Road. Just past the little rise is the Ira Allen Cemetery on land formerly owned by the Allen families. Ira Allen actually died in Philadelphia.

MANCHESTER AND SURROUNDING TOWNS (INCLUDES DORSET, RUPERT, PERU, WINHALL, LANDGROVE)

This is a part-driving, part-walking tour. The traveler can walk around Manchester Village, take a car to the other sites in Manchester (numbers 8–14) and then head to the other five towns. In Manchester, the Equinox Hotel, Hildene, Yester House and Manchester Village are on the National Register of Historic Places. In Dorset, the entire district around the Cephas Kent Inn is on the National Register of Historic Places.

MANCHESTER

1. Equinox Hotel

The Equinox Hotel had its start as the Marsh Tavern, which was located at the southernmost wing of the current hotel. The Equinox Hotel is on the National Register of Historic Places and is the culmination of combining several hotels over the last two hundred years. The orientation of the Marsh Tavern, with its south entrance, would have had the same orientation as the current southern wing. In 1775–77, Union Street went through where the enclosed walkway on the first floor of the hotel is now located. This is where Mary Todd Lincoln stayed in 1864, acquainting her oldest son, Robert Todd

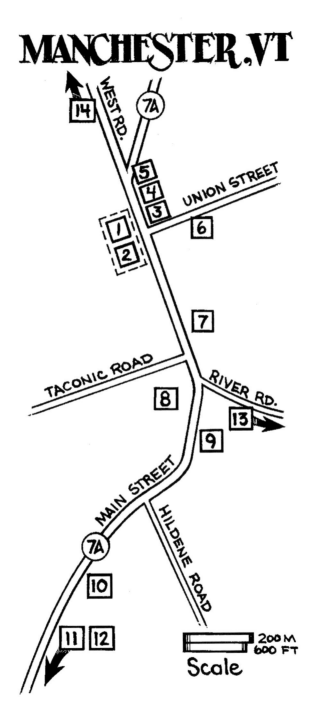

MANCHESTER MAP
Significant sites of interest for the events of 1775 and 1777.

THE EQUINOX HOTEL, MANCHESTER
The roots of the hotel date back to 1769 with the Marsh Tavern. The Marsh Tavern was located on the foundation where the far left section (south end) of the current hotel exists today.

Lincoln, with Manchester and Vermont. He was later to build his ancestral home, Hildene, in Manchester.

2. Marsh Tavern (Equinox Hotel)

The original Marsh Tavern (see image on page 70) was built in 1769, which is the basis for the Equinox Hotel claim, "Established 1769." The Marsh Tavern was a plain, wooden building less than two full stories high, standing with its side to the road. The original ground floor consisted of two rooms of about the same size, a kitchen in the rear of these rooms extending from the south end of the building and a pantry north of the kitchen. The main entrance was nearly in the center of the building and opened into the south front room. From this room, a door opened into the kitchen, and in the south end of the kitchen was the stairway leading to the upper story. On this floor were two small rooms in the rear, a large front chamber in the south end of the building and a smaller one in the north end.

This tavern is rich in history for Manchester and, for that matter, the United States. Marsh himself also had a house in Dorset. The Green Mountain Boys met here, as did the Vermont Council of Safety in July 1777, when it decided to seize Tory properties to finance troops. This was the first instance of property confiscation in the United States. The Continental Congress, in late 1777, recommended that all the colonies follow this Vermont model. The Marsh Tavern and the French property across the street (now 1811 House) were seized because Jeremiah French and William Marsh were Tories. Jeremiah French was William Marsh's father-in-law. William Marsh seems to have moved to Dorset in the spring of 1777. Although a supporter of the Revolution at first, he rode to the British army in July 1777. Marsh was permitted to return, and he lived and died in Dorset.

It was also here where the Council of Safety sent out a letter to New Hampshire asking for help against the British troops who were now in Castleton. John Stark answered the call and came with his troops.

SOLDIERS MONUMENT ON THE VILLAGE GREEN, MANCHESTER
Names of soldiers from Manchester who fought in wars before 1905 are inscribed on the base. It was built with public donations. The stones were cut and shaped by W.H. Fullerton. In the background is the 1811 House.

3. Bennington County Courthouse

The courthouse was built after the Revolutionary War. It was built on the original cemetery that also extended over to adjacent Union Street. The cemetery contained the remains of Revolutionary War heroes. The cemetery was moved south in Manchester in 1791 to become the Dellwood Cemetery. Bennington County is the only county in Vermont with two court towns or "shires" (Bennington and Manchester); hence the reference to Bennington County as the "Shires of Vermont."

4. Soldier's Monument

This granite monument features a Continental soldier (probably not Ethan Allen, although Allen did wear epaulets) with a sword and determined expression. It contains the names of Manchester people who fought in the wars prior to 1905. The monument was cut and shaped by W.H. Fullerton of Manchester Center and built with public donations. Note the symbolic placement of the soldier facing west, not north or south, toward New York.

On the Revolutionary War plaque, note the name of Nathan Beman. He was the teenager who guided Allen into Fort Ticonderoga. He returned to Manchester and married a Manchester woman. He is pictured with Ethan Allen on page 49. Also note Gideon Ormsby's name. He was a captain in the Green Mountain Boys, and Ormsby Hill was named after him.

Note the Robertses' names. John and his three sons (Christopher, Benjamin and John Jr.), who lived in Manchester, were with Ethan Allen at the capture of Fort Ticonderoga. Christopher was one of the first to enter the fort. Peter and John Jr. were at the battle of Bennington. Christopher had taken the women and children into Massachusetts in 1777 for protection from the British and had just gotten into Massachusetts when he heard of the victory and returned.

For real trivia, in the movie *Baby Boom* (1980s) with Diane Keaton, she is shown peddling her gourmet baby food in front of the monument.

In a general sense, this spot shows the natural dividing spot. Although there were some cutover roads in 1775, Manchester represented a real choice for the expedition going to capture Fort Ticonderoga. There is the route to the right following Route 7A, then 7 north to Rutland and then over to Fort Ticonderoga. The other route is straight ahead down West Road, north through the Mettewee Valley and eventually to Fort Ticonderoga. The marchers took the latter route, probably because it was faster.

1811 HOUSE, MANCHESTER.
Originally built in 1770, it became an inn in 1811, hence the name. Jeremiah French, who became a Tory just before the Battle of Bennington, owned it. He also owned another house on Main Street. It is now operated as an inn.

5. 1811 House (1770)

The inn was actually a farm property owned by Jeremiah French, whose property was seized for being a Tory. Ironically, French was one of the original settlers of Manchester from New York. French fled to Canada and died there. Although built around 1770, it was named the 1811 House because, in

1939, Henry Robinson made it into a hotel again and reverted back to the 1811 name. French also owned another house in Manchester (see number 10). On the trivia side, Charles Isham made this his home in the early 1900s. Charles Isham's wife was Mary "Mamie" Lincoln Isham, Abraham Lincoln's granddaughter and future heir to Hildene, the Lincoln family home in Manchester

6. Stark Viewing Spot

Walk down Union Street east about a hundred yards. Look directly ahead to the break in the Green Mountains. That is where Bourne Brook comes down Downer Glen. John Stark came over the mountains, through Peru and Winhall and into Manchester on this route. He then crossed the valley to the left and went to number 14, the campgrounds at what is now the Southern Vermont Arts Center. Looking to the left, Bromley Mountain ski area can be seen. Bromley Brook comes down from Peru in this area. Stark's troops may have also taken this route. The land at this spot was once owned by Mesheck Weare, president of New Hampshire, who responded to Vermont's request for help by sending John Stark.

7. Millet-Hoyt House

This is one of the oldest existing homes in the village. Originally owned by Lucius Barnard and used as a blacksmith and harness shop, it is actually two houses together. The north part of the two homes may have been the residence and the other the shop. This was not here on the march to Fort Ticonderoga, but it was here in 1777. It is now a private residence.

8. Warner Campground (1777)

It was from here on August 15 that the Green Mountain Boys, in the rain, began their march to Bennington to save the second engagement at the battle of Bennington. It is believed that Warner was already in Bennington, and Samuel Safford was the leader. There is written reference supporting the location of the campground as being above where River Road meets Historic 7A. There is logic to this, as Weller's Tavern is nearby, it is on a main road and there is a stream for water nearby that cuts down through what is now Dellwood Cemetery. An old map also places the campground here. It was reported that an axe was found here. Also, there is reference to the campground being south of the Equinox Hotel near the "Swift" farm. It was also near the Marsh Tavern for meetings. Some say it might even have been on the east side of 7A (it could have been on both sides as well). Initially, it was indicated that Herrick's Rangers made their camp "adjacent to" Warner's camp.

9. Eliakem Weller Tavern

Built before 1774, this was perhaps the first inn in Manchester Village. It became popular as "Anna Weller's." On March 2, 1774, it was the site of a convention declaring cooperative protection of New Hampshire Grant settlers from New York settlers. At the March 1774 meeting, it was decided to be ready to go to defense on short notice. Weller's daughter married one of the Roberts brothers, who went to Fort Ticonderoga with Ethan Allen (see picture page 31). It is now a private residence.

10. Jeremiah French House

The main front part of the house was built at least as early as 1774 (see picture on page 74). The house was owned by Jeremiah French, one of the largest landowners and first settlers of Manchester. It has an attractive and distinctive "hip roof" design. Jeremiah French became a Tory and joined the Queen's Loyal Rangers on July 5, 1777, just as Burgoyne was about to capture Fort Ticonderoga. He was in the Battle of Bennington, was captured and was taken to Bennington for processing after the battle. He would later be freed as part of a prisoner exchange and then lived in Canada as a respected citizen (see also number 5). His daughter married William Marsh. Currently owned by Martha and Richard Heilmann, they have preserved the look of this beautiful hip-roofed house.

11. Inn at Ormsby Hill

About a mile south on Historic 7A is the Inn at Ormsby Hill. The front part of the inn was built in 1770 or sooner. The inn also indicates that it can't be confirmed, but Ethan Allen may have stayed there. There are also remains, including bars, of a jail in the basement. The land and home were owned at one time by Edward Isham, who changed the name of Purdy Hill to Ormsby Hill. Gideon Ormsby was a Green Mountain Boy. Land in back of the inn was eventually sold by the Isham family to Robert Todd Lincoln (Abraham Lincoln's son) so he could build his ancestral home, Hildene.

INN AT ORMSBY HILL, MANCHESTER
This inn was built in 1770, or even as early as 1764. Tradition says that Ethan Allen stayed here. Soldiers going north or south in 1775 or 1777 would have passed this home as it was on a main route. It currently operates as an inn.

12. Samuel Rose House

About a mile south on Historic 7A from the Inn at Ormsby Hill is the old Samuel Rose farm, which is now Wilcox Dairy properties. Turn right at Wilcox Dairy and go about a hundred yards to the end of the road. The road that crosses at the T is the old Route 7. Rose was one of the early settlers of Manchester. Still visible as the north end of the main farmhouse on the old Historic Route 7, the house was built circa 1769. The farm would have been visible to the marchers north and south from Fort Ticonderoga and may have been a camping ground for Revolutionary War soldiers. It is now a private house.

ETHAN ALLEN DAYS, MANCHESTER
Ethan Allen Days are held annually at Hildene Meadowlands and include exhibits, educational programs, reenactments and other events. *Courtesy of Friends of Hildene, Inc. Photo by Lee Krohn.*

13. Hildene Meadowlands

About a mile down River Road from Historic 7A is Hildene Meadowlands. This meadow is where the reenactments have taken place as part of Ethan Allen Days celebrations. About thirty feet past the first opening in the stone wall is the place where Peggy Lincoln Beckwith (Abraham Lincoln's great-granddaughter) had her hangar (see image on page 54). Parts of the cement foundation are still visible. Peggy flew Ethan Allen IV over the dedication ceremony for Ethan Allen Highway in 1930 from Bennington to Manchester.

14. Stark's Campgrounds, Southern Vermont Arts Center (Yester House)

About a mile down West Road from the Equinox Hotel is the Southern Vermont Arts Center. Although not visible from the entrance road, these springs did provide water years ago, as did the stream coming down from Mount Equinox and crisscrossing the road. Farther up are more springs near the Yester House. Not only did this area have water, but it was also on the main road north (West Road) at the time and was about a mile from the Marsh Tavern. A lot of the water in the area has dried up.

DORSET/RUPERT

From Manchester you can go out to Rupert via Dorset and then return to Manchester via East Dorset for a nice loop.

Manchester West Road starts at Manchester Village. At the other end of West Road is Route 30 (Seth Warner Memorial Highway). Take a left on Route 30 (Seth Warner Memorial Highway) and then another left after about half a mile onto Dorset West Road, which was the main road north in this area in 1775.

Ethan Allen Spring

Located opposite a beautiful orchard on Dorset West Road, north of the two-story marble house and gardens, is the Ethan Allen Spring. Tradition says that Ethan Allen used this spring while camping on his was to capture Fort Ticonderoga in 1775. The state register indicates that it has been used as a local watering hole since 1770. There is no solid documentation on file to support this claim. It is now on private property about twenty feet off West Road. As you approach the spring on West Road, you will see a big wetlands area into which the spring feeds.

Kent Tavern/Kent Inn/Marker

Just up the road from the Ethan Allen Spring is the Cephas Kent Inn with a stone marker in front. Besides being pretty, the Kent District, as

KENT DISTRICT MARKER AND
KENT INN, DORSET
The marker indicates that
the Cephas Kent Dwelling
was where Seth Warner was
elected head of the Green
Mountain Boy regiment and
where a convention decided
that the New Hampshire
Grants would be a "separate
district (state)." The Cephas
Kent Inn behind was built
circa 1773. The inn is now a
private residence.

this area is known, had significant events occur in American history. At the tavern in July 1775, a convention of elders (not all Green Mountain Boys) elected Seth Warner as colonel in a new Continental Regiment of Green Mountain Boys. Two years later, Warner, as head of the same group, would be a hero at the Battle of Hubbardton on July 7, 1777, and then a month later, leading almost the same troops, he would be a hero of the Battle of Bennington. This spot is also where, in 1776, three months after the United States declared its independence, Vermont declared its independence and became "a separate district (state)."

The still-standing Cephas Kent Inn is indicated as being built circa 1773. There was a tavern nearby that no longer exists. There are ongoing discussions about the age of the Cephas Kent Inn and whether it was a separate "dwelling" or home.

Kent Meadows
Across from Kent Inn is Kent Meadows, which "legend" and "tradition" say is where Ethan Allen and the Green Mountain Boys camped on their way to capture Fort Ticonderoga. From diaries, it is pretty clear that some marchers came through here, but not at the same time. The actual camping could have occurred between the Ethan Allen Spring and what are the Kent Meadows now.

Mile Marker
Up the road about five hundred yards, on the corner Old Orchard and West Roads, there was a stone mile marker indicating that Bennington was twenty-nine miles(XXIX M.B.) to the south. For protection and historical

preservation, it was removed and placed in the Dorset Historical Society for viewing. The exact date of placement of this marker is not known, as dates range from 1775 to 1800. Whether this mile marker was there when the marchers were going to Fort Ticonderoga is not important.. The important thing is that it shows that this was a well-traveled route and needed to be marked.

Amos Field House
A little north on West Road is Foote Road. At the top, you will see a remodeled circa 1775 house, again indicating that homes existed along this route. It is believed that this higher road was the original road in the area. The house is now a private residence.

RUPERT/DORSET
Continue on Foote Road, which leads back to West Road. Keep going a few yards. This is now Rupert. Some of the troops in 1775 may have gone east (now 153) over the mountain, but most likely they went out Route 30 to East Rupert.

Harmon Mint (Hagar Brook)
About a mile north on Route 30 there is a state marker on the right by a little turnoff indicating the site of the Harmon Mint. This is Hagar Brook, formerly Mill Brook, which is where Jonathan Eastman had a log cabin around 1767. Route 30 used to be a Native American trial, but it eventually became an important road during the Revolutionary War. Ethan Allen was with the group here that was going to Fort Ticonderoga. We don't know exactly where they met, but it could have been on Route 30, heading out the Mettawee Valley to Pawlet.

Oldest Quarry
If you decide not to drive out the spectacularly preserved Mettewee Valley to Pawlet (in Rutland County), go back south on Route 30 to and through Dorset. You will pass the 1796 Dorset Inn and the Dorset village green. Farther south is the marble quarry on the left. The sign indicates that it is "the oldest quarry" in the United States. As trivia, the massive solid columns for the DAR's Continental Hall in Washington were taken from the quarry just behind the one adjacent to Route 30. The quarries are on private property.

Deacon John Manley House

Just south of the quarry on Route 30 is a marble house, which had its beginnings around 1773 for Deacon John Manley. This was not the main road in 1775, but there is an indication of some houses being in the area. This private home may be the first marble house in Vermont.

Continuing south on Route 30, Morse Hill Road is on the left. Make a left and go over the foothill of Mount Aeolus. Going over Morse Hill Road will give a sense of how the mountain splits Dorset and the roads to the north. One can travel on the west side of Mount Aeolus out Route 30 to Fort Ticonderoga or one can go north on Historic 7A and Route 7 to the east to Fort Ticonderoga via Rutland. You will come out at Route 7 in East Dorset.

Deming House

At the intersection of Route 7A and Morse Hill Road is the Deming House, probably built a few years after 1777. The land, however, was apparently owned by William Marsh, Deming's half brother. It has been stated that General Arthur St. Clair stayed in East Dorset at "the house of William Marsh" on July 8 and wrote a letter to General Schuyler. St. Clair had just come down what is now Route 7 from Rutland after the battle at Hubbardton. It is not known exactly where, but there must have been a William Marsh home nearby. Marsh, a Tory, came back to Dorset and is buried in Dorset. The house is a private residence.

Route Historic 7A goes back into Manchester.

LANDGROVE/WINHALL/PERU

This is not a loop tour, as you will be going out and returning over the same basic road. It is best to start at Landgrove and come back to Manchester. Route 11 goes east out of town toward the ski areas. After about ten miles, Route 11 passes the Bromley Ski Area. After another two or three miles, there is turnoff for Peru. Just past the village of Peru is Hapgood Pond Road. After about five miles Hapgood Pond Road enters Landgrove and ends at Old Country Road and Landgrove Road.

Utley Flats (Landgrove)

Stark came down into Bennington County on what is now Old County Road and, after turning around and looking back west, he crossed the open area known as Utley Flats. Returning back over Utley Flats, there are several houses on the right.

Captain Utley's Farm (Landgrove)

According to local historians, the yellow house with the attached barn has as its roots Captain Utley's farm, where some of Stark's troops stopped. Tradition says that Captain Utley is buried on the farm, but his remains have not been found. It is now a private residence.

STARK MONUMENT, PERU
The statue indicates where John Stark camped on August 6, 1777, on his way to Bennington for the Battle of Bennington.

Peru Stark Campground Monument

From Captain Utley's Farm to the Stark Statue is about five miles on Hapgood Pond Road. The actual route of Stark was probably a little to the north of Hapgood Pond Road through what is now Hapgood Pond Recreation area. Stark came out at what is now North Road and then continued to Hapgood Pond Road. This monument is where Stark camped on August 6, 1777, on his way from New Hampshire to Manchester and the Battle of Bennington. There was spring water available near this spot. A report in 1891 states that some troops may have gone a little farther west to camp past the village of Peru. Over a thousand soldiers came through here.

French Hollow (Winhall)

Hapgood Pond Road continues back through the village of Peru to Route 11. From Route 11 West back to the Bromley Ski area is about two or three miles. Just past the Bromley Ski Area, on the rise, is a spectacular view of Winhall. Stark's troops had apparently come down from Peru and cut across about three or four miles out through the area called French Hollow and then headed west toward Downer Glen and down into Manchester. Some troops may have taken the Bromley Brook route, which would have been a little north of Route 11 as it goes back down to Manchester.

STARK'S ROUTE TO BENNINGTON FROM NEW HAMPSHIRE

For those interested in following the entire route taken by General Stark from New Hampshire to his incredible victory at the Battle of Bennington, you can combine tours.

Starting at Charleston, New Hampshire (Fort at No. 4), the basic route taken by Stark was close to the current Route 11 through Chester, Vermont. Two miles past Londonderry is Landgrove Road, which goes north into Landgrove. There, Landgrove Road meets Old County Road and Hapgood Pond Road. The Landgrove/Winhall/Peru section of the Manchester tour ends in Manchester, as does Route 11. (There are no roads now down Downer Glen.) From Manchester, reverse the Bennington to Manchester tour and take Route Historic 7A to Bennington. At the Catamount Tavern in Bennington, explore Old Bennington with the Old Bennington tour. Use the map for the Bennington Battle Theater tour to visit the sites outside Old Bennington, including Stark's encampment (August 14–16), from which he launched his attack on the British on August 16.

TIMELINE

*Key Events Affecting Bennington County in the Capture of
Fort Ticonderoga and in the Battle of Bennington*

1741	Benning Wentworth becomes governor of New Hampshire.
1749	Using the Crown's decision to make New Hampshire responsible for Fort Dummer (west of the Connecticut River) and other precedents, Wentworth claims authority to charter towns west of the Connecticut River all the way to twenty miles east of the Hudson River. The first town west of the Connecticut River chartered was Bennington. This starts a dispute with New York, which claimed lands east to the Connecticut River.
1770	Ethan Allen forms the Green Mountain Boys in Bennington to use paramilitary techniques to resist New York land claims. By now, Wentworth has chartered over one hundred towns.
1770–1774	Many skirmishes between New Hampshire Grant holders and New York land claimants occur. The Crown has not resolved the issue.
1775	**April 19** Lexington and Concord. Rebellion against the Crown begins.
	May 5 Ethan Allen leaves Bennington to march north and muster Green Mountain Boys.
	May 10 Ethan Allen and the Green Mountain Boys capture Fort Ticonderoga from the British for the first American victory of the Revolutionary War. This was the first offensive action against the British empire.
1776	**July 4** United States declares independence from Great Britain.
	September New Hampshire Grants, in Dorset, declare themselves a "separate district(state)."

1777 **July 6** Americans evacuate Fort Ticonderoga and Mount Independence with the threat of a British invasion force of about seven thousand troops moving south down Lake Champlain Valley.

July 7 The British pursue retreating Americans. They are stopped by Seth Warner at the Battle of Hubbardton, Vermont.

July 8 Vermont (contraction of French words for "green" and "mountain") adopts its constitution.

July 10 The British send German mercenaries back to Castleton, Vermont, threatening invasion of Bennington County and New England.

July 11 Meetings in Marsh Tavern, Manchester. The Council of Safety pleads for help from New Hampshire and others. The Council of Safety also decides to raise money by seizing Tory property and selling it.

August 7 John Stark arrives in Manchester with over one thousand troops. He tells American General Lincoln that he is not going to Saratoga, but is going to stay in Vermont, where he thinks the British will attack supplies at Bennington.

August 8 Stark leaves for Bennington.

August 9–13 Stark camps at the foot of Mount Anthony, Bennington.

August 14 Stark moves his camp to Harrington Road, Bennington, almost within sight of a British foraging party.

August 15 Word reaches the Green Mountain Boys' reinforcements in Manchester that they are needed in Bennington. They break camp and march to Bennington in the rain.

August 16 Now with about two thousand troops (including Massachusetts, Vermont and New Hampshire militia), Stark attacks British forces. Seth Warner and the Green Mountain Boys arrive in time to help defeat the British reinforcements, achieving resounding American victory at the Battle of Bennington. There are seven hundred prisoners and two hundred dead for the British out of a total of one thousand; American casualties out of about two thousand were about thirty dead and forty wounded. Prisoners were taken to Bennington's first meetinghouse.

October 17 Without supplies and the troops lost at Bennington (about 15 percent of his troops), Burgoyne surrenders. France and others enter the war. This was the turning point of the war.

LONGITUDE AND LATITUDE COORDINATES FOR GPS USERS

The latitude and longitude coordinates were taken from public documents in historic site registers or were taken by the author. The author took coordinates at the nearest public spot (e.g., a road) to view the site. As indicated in the text, please respect that some of these sites are in private hands. Many of these sites are so near each other that the accuracy of consumer GPS systems makes them appear to overlap.

OLD BENNINGTON

		Latitude	Longitude
1	Catamount Tavern Site	42°53′06″	73°12′49″
2	Catamount Monument	42°53′10″	73°12′50″
3	Ethan Allen Homesite/Marker	42°53′02″	73°12′47″
4	Old Burying Ground	42°53′01″	73°12′47″
5	Old First Church	42°53′00″	73°12′46″
6	Village Green Marker	42°53′00″	73°12′46″
7	Jedediah Dewey House	42°52′57″	73°12′46″
8	Nathaniel Brush House	42°52′58″	73°12′46″
9	Walloomsac Inn	42°53′00″	73°12′46″
10	Isaac Tichenor House	42°52′57″	73°12′53″
11	Samuel Robinson Cabin Marker	42°53′10″	73°12′50″
12	John Stark Statue	42°53′22″	73°12′56″
13	Bennington Battle Monument	42°53′22″	73°12′58″

14	Seth Warner Memorial	42°53'18"	73°12'54"
15	Nichols and Symonds Markers	42°53'20"	73°12'58"
16	Continental Storehouse Marker	42°53'21"	73°12'58"
17	Bennington Museum	42°53'00"	73°12'34"
18	Mile Marker	42°52'30"	73°12'49"
19	Kelly House	42°50'59"	73°12'09"
20	Samuel Safford House (Inne)	42°52'44"	73°11'10"
21	USS *Bennington* Bell	42°52'39"	73°11'49"

BENNINGTON BATTLE THEATER

		Latitude	Longitude
1	Catamount Tavern Site	42°53'06"	73°12'49"
2	Continental Storehouse Marker	42°53'21"	73°12'58"
3	Scott House	42°53'14"	73°14'15"
4	Hubbell House	42°52'47"	73°14'15"
5	Dimmick's Tavern	42°52'38"	73°15'29"
6	Harmon Inn	42°53'51"	73°15'01"
7	Breckenridge Farm	42°54'34"	73°14'58"
8	Warner's Homesite	42°54'37"	73°15'12"
9	Henry House	42°54'42"	73°15'16"
10	Henry Bridge Crossing	42°54'45"	73°15'16"
11	Stark's Second Camp	42°55'31"	73°16'00"
12	Molly Stark Speech Site	42°55'32"	73°16'00"
13	Bennington Battlefield	42°56'01"	73°18'17"
14	Baum House	42°58'13"	73°16'09"

BENNINGTON TO MANCHESTER (ABOUT TWENTY-TWO MILES)

Bennington

	Latitude	Longitude
Harwood Hill	42°54'35"	73°12'35"

Shaftsbury

	Latitude	Longitude
Robert Frost House	42°56'04"	73°12'35"

	Latitude	Longitude
Munitions House	42°56'44"	73°12'24"
Waldo House	42°58'73"	73°12'25"
David Galusha Inn	42°58'54"	73°12'24"
White Column Stable	42°58'44"	73°12'25"
Waldo Tavern Site	42°58'41"	73°12'25"
1769 House	42°59'13"	73°12'23"
Carpenter House	42°58'33"	73°14'01"
Jonas Galusha House	42°59'17"	73°12'23"

Arlington

	Latitude	Longitude
Hawley-Crofut House	43°04'33"	73°09'56"
Ethan Allen Cemetery	43°04'28"	73°09'15"
Remember Baker Plaque	43°03'35"	73°08'21"
Tory House	43°03'35"	73°08'23"
Ethan Allen Homesite	43°04'18"	73°09'12"
Tory Lane	43°04'31"	73°09'44"

Sunderland

	Latitude	Longitude
Ira Allen House	43°06'53"	73°07'22"
Ira Allen Cemetery	43°06'46"	73°07'12"

MANCHESTER

(PLUS DORSET, RUPERT, LANDGROVE, WINHALL, PERU)

Manchester (From Manchester Tour Map)

		Latitude	Longitude
1	Equinox Hotel	43°09'42"	73°04'19"
2	Marsh Tavern	43°09'42"	73°04'19"
3	County Courthouse	43°09'43"	73°04'19"
4	Memorial Monument	43°09'45"	73°04'19"
5	1811 House	43°09'46"	73°04'19"
6	Viewing Spot	43°09'43"	73°04'12"
7	Hoyt House	43°09'33"	73°04'20"
8	Warner Campground	43°09'21"	73°04'22"

9	Weller Tavern	43°09'20″	73°04'23″
10	Jeremiah French House	43°09'11″	73°12'49″
11	Inn at Ormsby Hill	43°08'36″	73°05'23″
12	Samuel Rose Farm	43°07'39″	73°05'52″
13	Hildene Meadowland	43°08'35″	73°04'18″
14	Stark Campground (SVAC)	43°10'31″	73°04'17″

Dorset

	Latitude	Longitude
Ethan Allen Spring	43°14'00″	73°05'30″
Kent Meadows	43°14'11″	73°05'50″
Cephas Kent Inn	43°14'15″	73°05'54″
Amos Field House	43°15'48″	73°07'11″
Manley Marble House	43°14'06″	73°04'59″
Demming House	43°13'44″	73°00'40″
Mile Marker Site	43°14'40″	73°06'20″

Rupert

	Latitude	Longitude
Intersection 153 Route 30	43°16'19″	73°07'29″
Hagar Brook	43°16'50″	73°07'32″

Landgrove

	Latitude	Longitude
Captain Utley's Farm	43°15'47″	72°51'41″
Utley Flats	43°15'53″	72°51'33″
Beginning of Stark Road	43°15'51″	72°49'51″

Peru

	Latitude	Longitude
Stark Campground Monument	43°13'57″	72°53'55″

Winhall

	Latitude	Longitude
View of Winhall	43°12'37″	72°56'17″

SUGGESTED FEDERAL, STATE AND PRIVATE HISTORIC SITES

Most of these sites have seasonal hours and require an admission fee. Please contact the sites for more information.

Bennington Battle Monument State Historic Site
Bennington, Vermont
www.historicvermont.org
The 306-foot monument has a visitor elevator and a visitor center is next to the monument. Visitors can drive around the monument year-round and see the associated monuments.

Bennington Battlefield State Historic Site
Walloomsac, New York
www.nyparks.com
Some of the engagements were outside of the park. The visitor center has nice aerial photography of the entire battle theater.

Carillon Cruises
Larrabees Point, Vermont
www.carilloncruises.com
Allows you to see Hand's Cove, Vermont, where Ethan Allen left to cross Lake Champlain.

The Fort at No. 4
Charleston, New Hampshire
www.fortat4.org
This is where John Stark mustered his troops before leaving for Bennington.

Fort Ticonderoga National Historic Landmark
Ticonderoga, New York
www.fort-ticonderoga.org
The fort has a museum, plus tours and other activities

Hubbardton Battlefield State Historic Site
Hubbardton, Vermont
www.historicvermont.com
This battleground is well-preserved, and there is a visitor's center.

Mount Independence State Historic Site
Orwell, Vermont
www.historicvermont.org
This site has well-preserved fortifications.

Saratoga National Historical Park
Stillwater, New York
www.nps.gov
The park is mostly open year-round, but contact for details. The Battle of Bennington was the prelude to the Battle of Saratoga, which many consider the turning point in the Revolutionary War.

GENERAL NOTES

1. Estimates of the population of Bennington County towns in 1775 were from Michael Bellesiles's book, *Revolutionary Outlaws: Ethan Allen and the Struggle for Independence on the Early American Frontier*, Appendix D. He indicates his sources and clearly states that they are estimates. Population estimates for the time, by their nature, are just that—estimates. In Michael Sherman's *Freedom and Unity*, it is estimated that Vermont's population in 1774 was twelve thousand to thirteen thousand, and Bellesiles's book had a population of about seventeen thousand in 1775. This indicates that Bellesiles's estimates may even be high. In any event, these numbers are small compared to the states of Massachusetts, Connecticut and New York.

2. Robert O. Bascom, after years of research in the early twentieth century, produced a list of the people who were with Ethan Allen at Fort Ticonderoga. The list is still not complete and it has been updated over the years. For instance, one earlier list did not include the name of Epaphras Bull. The original list identified about 125 people as being with Ethan Allen at Fort Ticonderoga. Most sources indicate that there were over 200 men with Ethan Allen at Hand's Cove, Vermont, on the shore of Lake Champlain on the early morning of May 10, 1775. Given that names are spelled differently and people moved around, it is an arduous task to uncover who was with Ethan Allen and where they actually lived. This list is available in *The Bulletin of the Fort Ticonderoga Museum* Vol. XIII (1977). The list is also available at the Bennington Museum and various other places.

3. The official name of Route 7A is Historic 7A.

4. There are no known paintings of Ethan Allen, Seth Warner or Remember Baker.

5. It is hoped that historic references do not offend people. For instance, even today many Vermonters feel that Vermont was never a "colony" of Great Britain. Therefore, there never was a colonial Vermont.

6. Spellings pose a problem in that some names and places have two, and sometimes more, spellings. Sometimes two spellings are correct in that a quote for a source spelling it one way is correct because that is how that person spelled it. Walloomsac is spelled many ways. Some write Skenesboro and some say Skenesborough. Even some monuments have different spellings. Also, "Kill" means river, so saying Batten Kill River is somewhat redundant. Locally, it is called the Batten Kill. However, literature also refers to it as the Batten Kill River.

7. Several other sources have been used such as the National Register of Historic Places documents for Bennington, Shaftsbury, Arlington, Manchester and Dorset. Personal interviews, maps, handwritten manuscripts, collections, compiled material from previous documents and so forth were also used. Organizations such as the United Empire Loyalists (UEL) in Canada were also helpful sources.

8. Much of the discussion of early Vermont came from Michael Sherman's (et al) *Freedom and Unity*, published by the Vermont Historical Society.

BIBLIOGRAPHY

Abenaki Nation. www.abenakination.org/

Aldrich, Lewis Cass. *History Bennington County, VT.* Syracuse, NY: D. Mason and Co., 1889.

Allen, Ethan. *The Narrative of Colonel Ethan Allen.* Cambridge, MA: Applewood Books, 1989.

Allen, Ira. *The Natural and Political History of the State of Vermont.* Rutland, VT: Charles E. Tuttle Publishers, 1969.

"Battle of Bennington, Historical New Hampshire." *New Hampshire Historical Society* 32, no. 4 (Winter 1977).

Bayhan, Richard S. *Historical Sketch of Buildings-Old Bennington.* Cleveland: Ohio Central Publishing Company, 1929. Original list by Deacon Samuel Chandler, 1870.

Beers Atlas. *Bennington County, VT 1869.* CD-ROM. Old Maps.

Bellesiles, Michael A. *Revolutionary Outlaws: Ethan Allen and the struggle for Independence on the Early American Frontier.* Charlottesville: University of Virginia Press, 1993.

Bird, Harrison. *March to Saratoga; General Burgoyne and the American Campaign 1777.* New York: Oxford University Press, 1963.

Borman, Lauri D. *Atlas of American History.* Skokie, IL: Rand McNally, 2005.

Bort, Mary Hart. *Manchester Memories of a Mountain Valley.* Tucson, AZ: Marshall Jones Company, Manchester Historical Society, 2005.

Brown, Charles Walter. *Ethan Allen of Green Mountain Fame.* Chicago: M.A. Donohue and Co., 1902.

Bulletin of the Fort Ticonderoga Museum, 1947–1983.

Burgoyne, Lt. General. *A State of the Expedition From Canada as Laid Before the House of Commons.* London: J. Almon, 1780.

Chapin, Carl M. *Manchester in Vermont History.* Manchester, VT: Manchester Historical Society, 1932.

Chartrand, Rene. *Ticonderoga 1758: Montcalm's Victory Against All Odds.* Oxford: Osprey Publishing, 2000.

Cheney, Cora. *Vermont: The State with the Storybook Past.* Shelburne, VT: Second New England Press, 1996.

Child, Hamilton. Gazetteer and Business Directory of Bennington County for 1880–1881. Syracuse, NY: Journal Office, 1880.

Chipman, Daniel. *Memoir of Colonel Seth Warner.* Panton, VT: Essence of Vermont, 2000.

Chittenten, Lucius E. *The Capture of Ticonderoga.* Rutland, VT: Tuttle and Co., 1872.

BIBLIOGRAPHY

Clark, Cameron. *The White Pine Series Architectural Monographs.* Vol. VIII, No. 5, *Houses of Bennington Vermont and Vicinity.* St. Paul, MN: White Pine Bureau, 1922.

Coffin, Charles C. *The Boys of '76.* Gainesville, FL: Maranatha Publications, 1998.

Coffin, Howard, Will Curtis and Jane Curtis. *Guns over the Champlain Valley.* Woodstock, VT: Countryman Press, 2005.

Collections of the Connecticut Historical Society. Vol. I, *1860: Papers Relating to the Expedition to Ticonderoga April and May.* Hartford: Connecticut Historical Society, 1775.

Collections of the Vermont Historical Society. Vol. I. Montpelier, VT: Printing and Publishing Committee, 1870.

Commanger, Henry Steele, and Richard B. Morris. *The Spirit of Seventy-Six: The Story of the American Revolution as Told by Participants.* New York: First Da Capo Press, 1995.

Congdon, Herbert Wheaton. *Old Vermont Houses.* New York: Alfred Knopf, 1946.

Cook, Flavius J. *Home Sketches of Essex County: Ticonderoga.* Keeseville, NY: W. Lansing and Son., 1858.

Crockett, Walter H. *Soldiers of the Revolutionary War Buried in Vermont.* Excepted from the *Proceedings of Vermont Historical Society 1903–04 and 1905–06.* Baltimore, MD: Genealogical Publishing, 1973.

Crannell, Karl. *John Stark—Live Free or Die.* Stockton, NJ: OTTN Publishing, 2007.

Davis, Kenneth S. "In the Name of the Great Jehovah and the Continental Congress." *American Heritage* XIV, No. 6 (October 1963): 65–77.

Deed Transfer for Building Site of Continental Storehouse. 1887. Russell Vermontiana Collection, Martha Canfield Library, Arlington, Vermont.

De Puy, Henry W. *Ethan Allen and the Green Mountain Heroes of '76.* New York: Phinney and Blakeman, 1861.

"Diary of a NH Soldier." *Bennington Banner,* August 20, 1930.

Dorset Vermont Bicentennial, Map and Legend. N.d. George A. Russell Collection of Vermontiana.

Drake, Samuel Adams. *Burgoyne's Invasion of 1777.* Cranbury, NJ: Scholar's Bookshelf, 2006.

Duffy, John J., Ralph H. Orth, J. Kevin Graffagnino and Michael Bellesiles. *Ethan Allen and his Kin.* Vol. I. Hanover, NH: University Press of New England, 1998.

Durnford, Lt. Engineer. *Position of the Detachment Under Lt. Col. Baum at Walmscock Near Bennington, August 16, 1777.* London: Wm. Faden, 1780.

Eagleston, H. *Equinox House Driving Map.* Chester, VT: The National Survey, 1892.

Filson, Brent. "The Warm and Winsome Walloomsac Inn." *Vermont Life* (Summer 1984): 8–11.

Fisher, Major General Carlton Edward, and Sue Gray Fisher Soldiers. *Sailors and Patriots of the Revolutionary War, Vermont.* Camden, ME: Picton Press, n.d.

Foster, Herbert D., and Thomas. W. Streeter. *Stark's Independent Command at Bennington.* Manchester NH: Standard Book Company, 1918.

Foulke, Patricia, and Robert Folk. *A Visitors Guide to Colonial and Revolutionary New England.* Woodstock, VT: Countryman Press, 2006.

Fritz, Jean. *Traitor.* New York: Putnam and Grosset Group, 1997.

Graffagnino, J. Kevin. *The Shaping of Vermont.* Rutland: Vermont Heritage Press, 1983.

Graffagnino, J. Kevin, and H. Nicholas Muller III. *The Quotable Ethan Allen.* Barre/Montpelier: Vermont Historical Society, 2005.

Gustafson, Peter. "A Lost Hero of the Green Mountain Boys: Remembering Remember Baker." *Bulletin of the Fort Ticonderoga Museum* XV, no. 1 (Winter 1988): 15–28.

Hahn, Michael T. *Ethan Allen: A Life of Adventure.* Shelburne, VT: New England Press, 1994.

Hall, Henry. *Ethan Allen: The Robin Hood of Vermont.* New York: D. Appleton and Co., 1892.

BIBLIOGRAPHY

Hall, Hiland. "Historical Readings," *State Banner*, 1841–42.

———. *History of Vermont.* Albany, NY: Joel Munsell, 1868.

Hall, S.R. *The Geography and History of Vermont.* Revised by Pliny White. Montpelier, VT: C.W. Willard, 1871.

Hamilton, Edward P. *Fort Ticonderoga: Key to a Continent.* Fort Ticonderoga, NY: Fort Ticonderoga, 1995.

Hemenway, Abby Maria. *Vermont Historical Gazetteer.* Vol. I. Burlington, VT: self-published, n.d.

Henry, Hugh. *Arlington Along the Battenkill: Its Pictured Past.* Arlington: Arlington Townscape Association, Inc., 1993.

"Herrick's Rangers," www.greenmountainrangers.com.

Hibbard, George S. *History of Rupert, 1761–1898.* Rutland, VT: Tuttle Co., n.d.

Hine, Marie Sheldon. "Collection of Rupert History, March 6, 2006." Bennington Museum, Vermont.

Historical Events Guide 2003. Wilmington, VT: Living History Association, 2003.

Holbrook, Stewart H. *Ethan Allen.* New York: Macmillan Co., 1940.

Houghton, Raymond C. *A Revolutionary Day Along Route 7.* Delmar, NY: CyberHaus, 2001.

Jellison, Charles A. *Ethan Allen: Frontier Rebel.* Syracuse, NY: Syracuse University Press, 1969.

Jennings, Isaac. Memorials of a Century: The Early History of Bennington, VT. Boston: Gould and Lincoln, 1869.

Jepson, George H. *Herrick's Rangers.* Bennington Museum Series No. 1. Bennington, VT: Hadwen, Inc., 1977.

Joslin, J., and B. Frisbie. *The History of Poultney.* Poultney, VT: Poultney Historical Society, n.d.

"Journal of Carleton and Burgoyne's Campaigns." Part II. *Bulletin of the Fort Ticonderoga Museum* XI, no. 6 (September 1965): 307–55.

Journal of Vermont Senate. Tuesday, February 27, 1996. JRH 92. www.leg.state.vt.

Ketchum, Richard M. *Saratoga.* New York: Henry Holt and Co., 1997.

Klyza, Christopher McGrory, and Stephen C. Trombulak. *The Story of Vermont: A Natural and Cultural History.* Hanover, NH: University Press of New England, 1999.

Lewis, Phebe Ann. *The Equinox, Est. 1769: Historic Home of Hospitality.* Manchester, VT: Johnny Appleseed Bookshop, 1993.

Lord, Philip, Jr. *War Over Walloomscoick.* Albany, NY: New York State Museum, 1989.

Lossing, Benson J. "Ethan Allen." *Harpers New Monthly Magazine* 102, no. 17 (November 1858).

———. *The Pictorial Field-Book of the Revolution.* New York: Harper and Brothers, 1860.

Martin, Fontaine. *The Landgrove Meeting House.* New Orleans: Louisiana Laborde Printing Co., 1981.

Maynard, Charles W. *Fort Ticonderoga.* New York: Rosen Publishing Group, 2002.

McKnight, Jack. "Ethan Allen, Philosopher." *Vermont Life* (Winter 1990).

Medcalfe, Mr. *A Map of Country in which the Army Under Lt. General Burgoyne Acted in the Campaign of 1777 and the Places of Principle Actions.* Engraved by William Faden. Charing Cross, London, 1780.

Merrill, John, VDS, and Caroline R. Merrill. *Sketches of Historic Bennington.* Cambridge, MA: Riverside Press, 1898.

Merrill, Perry H. *Vermont Under Four Flags.* Montpelier, VT: Northlight Studio Press, 1975.

Moore, Howard Parker. *A Life of General John Stark of New Hampshire.* New York, 1949.

Mott, Edward. "Journal of Capt. Edward Mott." *Collections of the Connecticut Historical Society* I (1860): 163–168.

Munson, Loveland. *The Early History of Manchester: An Address Delivered in the Music Hall on December 27, 1875*. Manchester, VT: Journal Print, 1876.

Neumann, George C. *Battle Weapons of the American Revolution*. Texarkana, TX: Scurlock Publishing, 1998.

Nickerson, Hoffman. *The Turning Point of the Revolution*. Boston: Houghton Mifflin, 1928.

Old First Church Historic Glimpse. Bennington, VT: Old First Church, n.d.

Page, John. "The Economic Structure of Society in Revolutionary Bennington." *Proceedings of the Vermont Historical Society* 49, no. 2 (Spring 1981).

Parks, Joseph, and the Bennington Museum. *The Battle of Bennington, August 16, 1777*. Bennington, VT: Bennington Museum, Inc., 2004.

Pell, John. *Ethan Allen*. Boston: Houghton Mifflin, 1929.

Peterson, Harold. *Encyclopedia of Firearms*. London: E.P. Dutton & Co., 1964.

Petersen, James E. *Seth Warner "This Extraordinary American."* Middlebury, VT: Dunmore House, 2001.

Phelps, Edward J. *One Day in August 1777*. Park McCullough House Association, n.d.

Rebok, Barbara, and Doug Rebok. *History of Bennington County*. Plus Printing Company, n.d.

Resch, Tyler. *Bennington's Battle Monument: Massive and Lofty*. Bennington, VT: Images from the Past, 1993.

———. *Dorset: In the Shadow of Marble Mountain*. West Kennebunk, ME: Phoenix Publishing for Dorset Historical Society, 1989.

———. *The Shires of Bennington*. Bennington, VT: Bennington Banner for the Bennington Museum, 1975.

Risch, Erna. *Supplying Washington's Army*. Washington, D.C.: Center of Military History, United States Army, 1981.

Rogers, Stillman D., and Rogers, Barbara Radcliffe. *Country Towns of Vermont*. Lincolnwood, IL: Country Roads Press, 1999.

Rose, Ben Z. *John Stark: Maverick General*. Waverly, MA: TreeLine Press, 2007.

Ross, John. "The Saga of Gentleman Johnny Burgoyne." *Vermont Life* 29, no. 2 (Winter 1974): 44–45.

Ruse, M. "General Stark and the Battle of Bennington." *Harper's New Monthly Magazine* 55 (June to November 1877).

Sage, James D. "The Old Topping Tavern." *Vermont Life* 25, no. 3 (1971): 42–47.

Shalhope, Robert E. *Bennington and the Green Mountain Boys*. Baltimore: Johns Hopkins University Press, 1996.

Sherman, Michael, Gene Sessions and P. Jeffrey Potash. *Freedom and Unity: A History of Vermont*. Barre, VT: Vermont Historical Society, 2004.

Smith, Donald A. Legacy of Dissent: Religious Politics in Revolutionary Vermont 1749–1784. PhD diss., Clark University, n.d.

Spargo, John. *Ethan Allen at Ticonderoga*. Rutland, VT: Tuttle Company, 1926.

Sparks, Jared. *The Life of Colonel Ethan Allen*. Burlington, VT: C. Goodrich and Co., 1858.

Stark, Caleb. *Memoir and Official Correspondence of Gen. John Stark*. Concord, NH: G. Parker Lyon, 1860.

Steegmann, Theodore, Jr. "New York Rangers in the Hampshire Grants, 1776–1777." *Vermont History: Proceedings of the Vermont Historical Society* 51, no.4 (Fall 1983).

Stout, Marilyn. "Vermont Walks: Village and Countryside." *Vermont Life* (1995).

Symonds, Craig L. *A Battlefield Atlas of the American Revolution*. Mt. Pleasant, SC: Nautical and Aviation Publishing Company of America, Inc., 1986.

Thompson, Judge D.P. *The Green Mountain Boys*. Weybridge, VT: Cherry Tree Books, 2000.

"USS *Bennington* Association." www.USS-Bennington.org.

Bibliography

"USS *Ethan Allen* Association." www.ssbn608.org.

Vermont, State of. *Historic Sites and Structures Survey*. Montpelier, VT: Division of Historic Preservation, n.d.

"Walking and Driving Tours of Dorset Vermont." Dorset Historical Society, 2004.

Wallace, Audrey. *Benedict Arnold: Misunderstood Hero?* Shippensburg, PA: Burd Street Press, 2003.

Walton, E.P., ed. *Records of the Council of Safety and Governor and Council of the State of Vermont, July 1775–1777*. Vol. I. Montpelier, VT: J. and J.M. Poland, 1873.

"Warner's Regiment." www.warnersregiment.com.

Whitelaw, James A. *Correct Map of the State of Vermont from Actual Survey*. Montpelier, VT: n.p., 1976.

Wilbur, James Benjamin. *Ira Allen: Founder of Vermont, 1751–1814*. Vol. I. Boston: Houghton Mifflin Co., 1928.

Wolfe, Virginia A., and Mary Bort. *Manchester Village Vermont: Walk on Marble to Points of Interest*. Manchester, VT: Manchester Historical Society, n.d.

Works Progress Administration for the State of Vermont, Federal Writers Project. *Vermont: A Guide to the Green Mountain State*. Cambridge, MA: Houghton Mifflin Co., 1937.

INDEX

INDEX